escape from the flames

How Ellen White grew from fear to joy

—and helped me do it too

Alden Thompson

Pacific Press® Publishing Association
Nampa, Idaho
Oshawa, Ontario, Canada
www.pacificpress.com

Designed by Michelle C. Petz
Cover photo © Getty Images

Copyright © 2005 by
Pacific Press® Publishing Association
Printed in the United States of America
All rights reserved

Unless otherwise noted, all Scripture quotations are from the New Revised Standard Version.

Additional copies of this book are available by calling toll-free 1-800-765-6955
or visiting http://www.adventistbookcenter.com

ISBN: 0-8163-2085-3

05 06 07 08 09 · 5 4 3 2 1

Dedicated to the little flock of faithful Adventists in Scotland.

Their deeply rooted faith and confident hope gave us an anchor when we needed it most.

Note: From 1972–1974, my wife, Wanda, and I lived in Scotland with our two daughters, Karin and Krista, while I was completing doctoral studies at the University of Edinburgh. The Edinburgh Church, with some forty members, was home, but the believers at Perth (seven first-generation Adventists), Dunfermline, and Dundee were also a source of inspiration and encouragement. Some five million people live in Scotland; less than three hundred are Adventists. We've been back many times since. The believers there continue to bless us, and we are grateful.

Contents

A Brief Word From the Author

You might expect a long story here at the beginning. Almost miraculously, I'm going to keep it short, very short. The reason is that the whole book is essentially a story—my story of how I have related to the life and writings of Ellen White.

I'm a very devout person, but also very curious. Had I been at the burning bush where Moses met God, my shoes would have come off immediately. But then I would have been bursting with eagerness to ask a question: "How did You do that?"

My deep love for God is His gift to me. So is my sense of curiosity. And for reasons which I cannot fully explain, the life and writings of Ellen White have helped me bring together the very different worlds of worship and curiosity. For that I am profoundly grateful. I know I am too fervent for some, too honest for others. And I'm sorry about that. But I really do want you to hear the story. I believe God gave His people a great and good gift when He called Ellen White to be His messenger. Tragically, we have often misused the gift. I'll have something to say about that, too, in this book. But *gratitude* is the word I want to loom larger than anything else.

I am also very much a people person. That's why my church is so important to me. I revel in every opportunity to come together with those who share the same hope—to laugh, to cry, to talk, to sing together, and sometimes even to whine together. My prayer is that this book will help us do all of that more and better—except maybe for the whining.

Now a brief warning: Chapter 6 is the exciting chapter. That's the one that tells how Ellen White escaped from hell—the doctrine of hell. But escaping from hell isn't easy. You have to go through five chapters before you're ready.

That's it. You didn't think I could be this short, did you? Let's get on with the story.

CHAPTER 1

Ellen White's Story— Briefly

If you and I were on a bus together and you had heard the name Ellen White for the very first time but wanted to know more, this is what I'd tell you:

Ellen Harmon White was a co-founder of the Seventh-day Adventist Church, a Protestant movement that developed in the aftermath of the great Millerite Disappointment of 1844.

Born in 1827 in Gorham, Maine, young Ellen suffered from very poor health in her childhood, mostly as a result of a stone thrown by a schoolmate that struck her in the face. That event ended Ellen's formal schooling.

Her family were devout Methodists who were attracted by the preaching of William Miller. Based on his study of the prophecies of Daniel, especially the 2,300-day prophecy of Daniel 8:14, Miller believed Jesus would return around 1843. He attracted a large following from a wide variety of denominations. By 1840, many Millerites began to be more specific in setting dates. October 22, 1844 became the focal point of great expectation—then turned into "The Great Disappointment."

Young Ellen was among those who continued to believe that God's hand was leading the Millerite movement. In December 1844, she received her first vision, a message of encouragement to the "little flock." When she continued to have visions, those Adventists who would eventually organize the Seventh-day Adventist Church came to the conclusion that God had given her the gift of prophecy in accordance with the New Testament promises in Ephesians 4 and 1 Corinthians 12. Thus her fellow believers confirmed her unique role in Adventism.

After the Disappointment, earnest Bible study led the group in formulating the "landmark" beliefs that would mark Adventist identity—the seventh-day Sabbath, the nearness of the Second Coming, the nonimmortality of the soul, and the understanding that the "cleansing of the sanctuary" of Daniel 8:14 referred to Christ's ministry in the heavenly sanctuary, not to an event on earth.

In 1846 Ellen married James White, another of the early Adventist pioneers. They had four sons.[1] Both James and Ellen played key roles in the events leading up to the formal organization of the Seventh-day Adventist Church in 1863. Describing how the two of them worked together in ministry, Ellen noted that her husband "would give a doctrinal discourse, then I would follow with an exhortation of considerable length, melting my way into the feelings of the congregation. Thus my husband sowed and I watered the seed of truth, and God did give the increase."[2] In spite of the poverty and illness that often dogged them in their early years, they worked tirelessly to advance the Advent cause.

In the early years of Adventism, Ellen White played a key role in spurring those developments that still are important in Adventism—publications, beginning in the late 1840s, health reform in the 1860s, education and missions in the 1870s. She remained active after her husband died in 1881, spending several years in Europe (1885–1887) and in Australia (1891–1900).

At two contentious and pivotal General Conference sessions—the "Righteousness by Faith" session of 1888 and the "Reorganization" session of 1901—she played a key role in urging her fellow Adventists to be more Christlike in their treatment of each other.

Today, Ellen White is perhaps best known for her writings, especially her counsels to the church and her devotional commentaries on Scripture.[3] Since her death in 1915, and in accordance with instructions laid down in her will, the Ellen G. White Estate makes her writings available to the church. Many topical compilations and daily devotionals have been published under the guidance of the Ellen G. White Estate. All of her published writings are now available on disk.

Ellen White's dominant role in Adventism continues to be deeply appreciated by many within the Adventist Church, vigorously discussed by all, and undoubtedly regretted by some. The questions that surface again and again are those that constitute the major reason for this book: How do her writings relate to the Bible? And how should the church and its members understand her "authority"?

---

[1] Henry (1847–1863), their oldest, died at age sixteen. James Edson (1849–1928) was rather wayward for a number of years, but ended up with a significant ministry among ex-slaves in the American South. William Clarence (1854–1937), usually known as Willie or W.C., played a more public role in Adventism, especially in connection with his mother's ministry after his father died in 1881. John Herbert, their fourth son, was born in 1860, but lived only a few months.

[2] *Testimonies for the Church*, vol. 1, p. 75 (1881).

[3] Many of her counsels to people and church groups, spanning the years 1855 to 1909, are included in the nine-volume set, *Testimonies for the Church*. Her five-volume devotional commentary on Scripture, the Conflict of the Ages series, continues to be popular, with *The Desire of Ages* (1898/1911) and *The Great Controversy* (1888) probably the best known. *The Desire of Ages* is the story of Jesus' life and ministry; *The Great Controversy* traces the continuing story of the conflict between good and evil from the time of Jesus' ascension to the final destruction of evil in the lake of fire. Her book *Education* (1903) continues to shape Adventist schools, and her other books on the life of Christ are also very popular: *Steps to Christ* (1892); her commentary on the Sermon on the Mount, *Thoughts From the Mount of Blessing* (1896); her book on Jesus' parables, *Christ's Object Lessons* (1900); and her commentary and health applications based on Jesus' healing miracles, *The Ministry of Healing* (1905).

CHAPTER 2

Which Side?

"I'm writing a book about Ellen White," I said.

"Which side?" he asked immediately.

"Positive!" I replied firmly, but noted that I really wanted to reach both sides—those who really love Ellen White and those who really don't; those who nearly worship her and those who wish she'd just go away. Go online on the Internet, and you'll discover what I mean; in a matter of moments both extremes are in your face.

The question, "Which side?" came from a lifelong Seventh-day Adventist. He had been an active leader in my church when I was a young pastor just starting out in ministry, and he's still active in the church. He knows about Ellen White. He knows the strong feelings that her name can stir. But he himself is not one of the passionate ones. He is in the middle. I want him, and the many like him, to benefit from this book too.

Finally, I also want to reach those for whom the name Ellen White is relatively new, including those who are mostly just curious. Now, if you're new to Adventism or if you just want to find out what makes Adventists tick, parts of this book may make you feel like you've landed in the middle of a family feud or perhaps in the middle of a family picnic. You'll feel awkward, like maybe you don't quite belong. I want you to know that I know you're there. I'll try to keep the in-house language to a minimum and explain the insider stuff as we go along.

In a sense, I'm preaching to the choir. But I'm twisting the meaning of that phrase just a bit, for this is a choir capable of great music. I hear snatches of it once in a while. But it's also a choir that can easily be tempted to quarrel instead of sing. I want to hear more singing and less quarreling. And in whichever group of readers you may fall, I'd be delighted if you could join the choir and help us sing.

With all that in mind, I want you to hear my vision for the "choir," the church, right here at the beginning. You'll see from Scripture and from Ellen White what makes me tick and why I am grateful for both.

My Vision for the Church

I don't know of anyone who likes the church just the way it is, not even its most tenacious supporters. All of us dream dreams about what the church *could* be. The trick is to dream dreams about a new and better church without alarming the saints in the "real" church that already exists. I'll summarize my vision for the church under five headings and then briefly note Ellen White's role in all this. For clarification, I should point out that when I say "church," I usually mean the Seventh-day Adventist Church, my church, though in many ways the basic principles would apply to the Old Testament "church," the New Testament "church," and to the larger Christian "church," thus including all those who follow Jesus.

1. **A church that helps people in need.** "Theology divides, but mission unites." I've heard that line from several sources, and from what I've seen, I believe it's true. But when I hear it or quote it, I always associate it with the person who first implanted it deeply enough in my soul to make it stick. That would be Jon Dybdahl, a good friend and the current president of Walla Walla College where I teach. He is a man of broad experience, who has spent extended time serving the church in Asia and in the United States, as well as having more brief exposure in other parts of the world.

Once alert to that principle regarding theology and mission, I've noted how easily devout believers can come together to work on projects focused on helping people. I've also noted how easily these same believers can fall to quarreling over matters of doctrine, theology, and biblical interpretation. Now, vigorous discussions over doctrine, theology, and our understanding of Scripture are crucial if the church is to stay strong and healthy. But such heavy mental exercises are not nearly so important as what the church does in a hands-on way to make a difference in the real world.

Key passages of Scripture point us in that direction. From the Old Testament we can quote the prophet Micah: "He has told you, O mortal, what is good; and what does the LORD require of you but to do justice, and to love kindness, and to walk humbly with your God?"[1] We can also quote the passage in Isaiah that Jesus used to define His mission for His hometown folk in Nazareth: "The spirit of the Lord GOD is upon me, because the LORD has anointed me; he has sent me to bring good news to the oppressed, to bind up the brokenhearted, to proclaim liberty to the captives, and release to the prisoners; to proclaim the year of the LORD's favor."[2]

And if you really want to be succinct, try Jesus' one-verse summary of the Old Testament: "In everything do to others as you would have them do to you; for this is the law and the prophets."[3] Closely related to that passage is His statement of the two great commands: " 'You shall love the Lord your God with all your heart, and with all your soul, and with all your mind.' This is the greatest and first commandment. And a second is like it: 'You shall love your neighbor as yourself.' On these two commandments hang all the law and the prophets."[4]

Two key features of this passage are often overlooked: First, Jesus is simply quoting the Old Testament. In other words, these commands are nothing new. Second, He gives us a hierarchy of values: Some things are more important than others. That sounds scary. But that's what Jesus taught, and that's what He lived. We'll be talking more about that.

Jesus sometimes got into trouble by putting the needs of particular people ahead of the requirements of particular laws. Read Matthew 12 for some good illustrations of how Jesus lived and how His opponents reacted. Because Jesus put people first, some traditionalists accused Him of being a lawbreaker. But Jesus did what He did because He was committed to the highest law of all. And when He defined that law in its double form—love to God and love for each other—He said that everything else "hangs" on these two. If a church would really take that saying of Jesus seriously, it would be the most unique church on earth. As difficult as that may sound, and as hard as it certainly is to put into practice, that was Jesus' dream for His people. I want that to be my dream and yours.

In that same connection, one other passage in the New Testament is very important: the parable of the judgment in Matthew 25:31–46, in which God puts all the "good" people with the sheep on the right, and everyone else with the goats on the left. Some are uncomfortable with this parable because it sounds suspiciously like salvation by works. But note that those who were commended by God for being "good" didn't even realize that they were doing good in any ultimate sense. They just went about helping those in dire need. They certainly weren't trying to impress God. In fact, His praise caught them by surprise.

One other thing worth noting about this parable is that the goats who go into "eternal punishment"[5] are not condemned for horrific deeds. They fall short simply because they failed to do good. That's rather sobering.

And we must not leave this passage without noting two Ellen White quotations from her remarkable commentary on it in *The Desire of Ages*. I have highlighted key words:

> Christ on the Mount of Olives pictured to His disciples the scene of the great judgment day. And He represented its decision as turning upon *one point*. When the nations are gathered before Him, there will be but two classes, and their eternal destiny will be determined by *what they have done or have neglected to do for Him in the person of the poor and suffering*.[6]

> Those whom Christ commends in the judgment may have *known little of theology, but they have cherished His principles*. Through the influence of the divine Spirit they have been a blessing to those about them. Even among the heathen are those who have *cherished the spirit of kindness;* before the words of life had fallen upon their ears, they have befriended the missionaries, even ministering to them at the peril of their own lives. *Among the heathen are those who worship God ignorantly, those to whom the light is never brought by human instrumentality, yet they will not perish.* Though ignorant of the written law of God, they have heard His voice speaking to them in nature, and have done the things that the law required. Their works are evidence that the Holy Spirit has touched their hearts, and they are recognized as the children of God.[7]

Ellen White's good words for the ignorant but kindly heathen remind me of another passage in the New Testament that startled me when I first really "heard" it. "If you know that he is righteous, you know that everyone who does what is right has been born of him."[8] Did you catch that? Born-again language, not for those who have knowingly accepted Jesus, the more usual way of using the phrase, but simply for those who do what is right. Remarkable!

So that's the first part of my vision for the church: getting on with the task of doing good. And whenever anyone anywhere on earth does good, the church ought to say a hearty "Amen."

2. **A church in touch with the real world.** In one technical sense of the word, Adventism came into existence as a "sect." That is, it was counter-cultural, just as the New Testament church was countercultural. In the first century A.D., Christians stood over against the dominant Greco-Roman culture, calling people to a higher walk with God. In short, they were swimming against the current.

Similarly, Adventism came into existence when most Christians were very optimistic about the future of this world, believing that the world was getting better and better and was on the verge of a new golden age of peace and prosperity. Adventists confronted that heady optimism, preaching the hard truth that the world was on the verge of destruction, that it had to be cleansed before it could be renewed. Adventists still hold to this truth about the future of the world.

But a danger lurks nearby for those who belong to a countercultural movement—the danger of isolation. In our eager longing for holiness, we can move so far away from the world that we end up living by ourselves and for ourselves. Then we easily become critical and grumpy, not very much like our Lord. To put it plainly, we can actually be of the world, but not really in it. I can't imagine that is what Jesus wants for us.

So I believe it's time for us to be more in touch with the world, to be in the world, but by God's grace, not contaminated by it. Two quotations from Ellen White have pointed me in this direction. First, to a brother heading into virgin territory in Africa she wrote:

> In laboring in a new field, do not think it your duty to say at once to the people, We are Seventh-day Adventists; we believe that

the seventh day is the Sabbath; we believe in the non-immortality of the soul. This would often erect a formidable barrier between you and those you wish to reach. Speak to them, as you have opportunity, upon points of doctrine on which you can agree. Dwell on the necessity of practical godliness. Give them evidence that you are a Christian, desiring peace, and that you love their souls. Let them see that you are conscientious. Thus you will gain their confidence; and there will be time enough for doctrines. Let the heart be won, the soil prepared, and then sow the seed, presenting in love the truth as it is in Jesus.[9] GW 119, 120 (1887 letter)

The other striking quotation was probably given as counsel to A. T. Jones, perhaps one of the most countercultural and confrontational Adventists alive at the end of the nineteenth century:

> The Lord wants His people to follow other methods than that of condemning wrong, even though the condemnation be just. He wants us to do something more than to hurl at our adversaries charges that only drive them further from the truth. The work which Christ came to do in our world was not to erect barriers and constantly thrust upon the people the fact that they were wrong.
>
> He who expects to enlighten a deceived people must come near to them and labor for them in love. He must become a center of holy influence.[10]

Now, if you are a cautious and conservative Adventist, those quotes may sound suspicious to you. But Ellen White really did write them. And if you want good biblical examples, consider Joseph, Daniel, Esther, and Nehemiah, all of whom gained the confidence of "outsiders," actually working for them, honestly and faithfully.

Given what I know of the "conservative" Adventist impulse (I have some of that blood in my veins), the mandate to Daniel is perhaps most impressive: The king had commanded that Daniel and his companions were to be "versed in every branch of wisdom" and "taught the literature and language of the Chaldeans."[11] As a result of their commitment to God, the Bible says that God gave these four young men knowledge and skill in every aspect of literature and wisdom.[12]

I believe it is possible for Christians in our day to experience that kind of exposure to the larger world. Some may need or want to follow the methods of A. W. Tozer, the well-known twentieth-century American preacher and author. When he felt the need to understand the works of William Shakespeare, "he read them through on his knees, asking God to help him understand their message."[13] I'm not suggesting that his approach should be standard. What I am suggesting is that we must find ways of being in touch with the real world and with God.

3. **A church that helps people with the business of daily living.** In the first point above, I was talking about people in dire need; here I'm talking about ordinary need. That's where most of us are most of the time.

John Wilson, editor of the Christian literary journal, *Books and Culture,* quoted an old Russian proverb from Aleksandr Solzhenitsyn's novel, *First Circle*: "It's not the sea that will drown you; it's the puddle." Wilson went on to say: "Most of us will not be martyrs. Instead, we will be caught up in a war of attrition: the war of everydayness."[14]

The church must be a place where we help each other cope with the business of living. And for Christians, that means living in hope.

4. **A church that brings different kinds of people together.** This may be the toughest challenge of all in our modern, individualistic world. We have less and less patience with things that don't meet our particular needs, and so we head for the door.

Because I teach at an Adventist college, my particular concern is how we deal with the broad spectrum, from those who have an urgent need to ask questions (the liberals) to those who have just as urgent a need to hold on to clear answers (the conservatives). Put another way, I dream of a church where both thinking and believing can take place. And let's be honest, some find it easier to think, while others find it easier to believe. I want a church that can help us on both counts.

One of the most remarkable Ellen White quotations in this respect comes from the beginning of the chapter, "In Contact With Others" in *The Ministry of Healing*. I first "heard" it from Arnold Kurtz, then a retired seminary professor (now deceased) when we were talking about the role of women in ministry. Later and quite independently of each other, an Adventist pastor and then an Adventist physician told me how this quotation had made a difference in their lives.[15] The physician had found it especially helpful when he was in mission service in Africa. Here is the quotation.

Every association of life calls for the exercise of self-control, forbearance, and sympathy. We differ so widely in disposition, habits, education, that our ways of looking at things vary. We judge differently. Our understanding of truth, our ideas in regard to the conduct of life, are not in all respects the same. There are no two whose experiences are[16] alike in every particular. The trials of one are not the trials of another. The duties that one finds light are to another most difficult and perplexing.

So frail, so ignorant, so liable to misconception is human nature, that each of us should be careful in the estimate we place upon another.[17] We little know the bearing of our acts upon the experience of others. What we do or say may seem to us of little moment, when, could our eyes be opened, we should see that upon it depended the most important results for good or for evil.[18]

5. A church in which all God's children can worship together. You will notice a fair bit of overlap in most of my dreams for my church. But each point has its purpose. Here I'm talking about a church which can call all God's people together for a common worship experience. I'm not saying that every worship experience should always include the whole community. In fact, the church is likely to be healthier (and the individual members happier) when we have smaller groups where kindred spirits can help each other as well as smaller groups where different kinds of people can work together on special projects. But we also need those special occasions when we all come together in all our diversity, the whole body of Christ together.

The toughest challenge here is probably the music. I suspect the Lord will have to tell us how to fix that when He comes. Still, we ought to find ways to come together, eat together, play together, pray together, yes, and even sing together. It will happen in the kingdom. Why not begin here?

The Role of Ellen White in "Church"

In this chapter I have talked about ideals, dreams, and visions—something beyond the present reality. I hope you have begun to sense something of the role Ellen White has played in shaping my vision for the church. In that connection, I really like the line from my former teaching colleague, Ernie Bursey, who is fond of saying, "Ellen White didn't just get visions, she gave them."

But if we are going to be of any earthly good, we have to move from vision to reality. And that is the story in the next chapter, "The Church and Ellen White." Prophetic voices are preserved by a "church," you see, by people who believe they have heard God's message through a human messenger. Without that community of believers, the prophet's voice would simply bounce off the canyon walls, echo for a few moments, and die.

The God-given process by which the community preserves the prophetic voice is one we too often overlook. Because we have so many Bibles, including special ones bound in leather and gold-stamped, we, too, easily forget that the voices preserved in those pages were at one time very fragile voices. Jeremiah and Jesus may be the most sobering examples.

In his own day, Jeremiah's message was so unpopular he was actually banned from the temple.[19] But God's people eventually realized that he was a true prophet. Under the guidance of the Spirit, God-fearing people brought together his sayings and writings, edited them, and produced what we now call the book of Jeremiah. In this case, Jeremiah didn't actually write it, even though it contains mostly his words.

As for the story of Jesus, what would have happened without the disciples? We have nothing in writing from Jesus Himself. It was the disciples who preserved His message. Because His words had changed them, they took His message out to change the world. And so we have the New Testament. And we have the New Testament only because of the church.

Ellen White's voice has been preserved by a similar process. Without a community who believed she was speaking God's word, her voice would have died. The church recognized and preserved her writings. And now her writings serve the church. The next chapter describes how and why that has made a difference in my life.

---

[1] Micah 6:8.

[2] Isaiah 61:1, 2; cf. Luke 4:18, 19.

[3] Matthew 7:12.

[4] Matthew 22:37–40.

[5] Matthew 25:46.

[6] *The Desire of Ages,* p. 637, emphasis supplied.

[7] *The Desire of Ages,* p. 638, emphasis supplied.

[8] 1 John 2:29, NIV.

[9] *Gospel Workers,* pp. 119, 120 (1915); *Evangelism,* p. 200; cf. "Letter to a Minister and His Wife Bound for Africa" (June 25, 1887 = Letter 12, to Elder Boyd; the almost verbatim "original" of the *Gospel Worker*s quote) in *Testimonies to Southern Africa,* pp. 14–20.

[10] *Testimonies for the Church,* vol. 6, pp. 121, 122; cf. Letter 59, 1900 (to A. T. Jones, April 18, 1900).

[11] Daniel 1:4.

[12] Daniel 1:17.

[13] Cited in "Tozer's Legacy," from A. W. Tozer, *The Pursuit of God* (Camp Hill, Pa.: Christian Publications, 1982, 1993 [1949]), p. 5.

[14] John Wilson, "Books and Culture," March/April 1997, p. 4.

[15] Rick Bowes, at the time, pastor of the Walla Walla City Church and Jack Hoehn, family practice physician in the Walla Walla valley.

[16] Original: "no two whose experience is alike."

[17] Original: "each should be careful in the estimate he places upon another."

[18] *The Ministry of Healing,* p. 483 (1905).

[19] See Jeremiah 36.

CHAPTER 3

The Church and Ellen White

The church preserves the prophetic voice so that the prophetic voice can serve the church. And if the church is following Jesus, the prophetic voice will make us more effective in serving the world. This is a story that illustrates that point from the perspective of my own experience with Ellen White. And that experience can be summarized very simply: Ellen White helped me study my Bible, then studying my Bible helped me in my study of Ellen White.

Now the rest of the story.

As I noted in the preface, I am very much a people person. I relish a lively discussion with any number of people, from one on up. I would be keenly disappointed if we all thought just alike, for then there would be nothing to discuss. But much worse than no discussion at all is quarrelsome discussion. And religious people can be the most quarrelsome of all. Paul's letters to the Corinthian church can give you all the illustrations you need of this, and probably more than you want.

To be perfectly honest, though, religion may not be the cause of our problems; it may simply highlight the problems as God begins the process of leading us to solutions. I've seen the religious impulse become a great blessing in healing individual lives and in bringing people together in community, especially when they are following Jesus. If the Corinthian church was a tangled mess (and it was), Paul's letter to the church at Philippi tells of people in love with the Lord, with each other, and with the world—all in the right sense of the word. What makes the difference? That's a question that interests me greatly.

Since I am a deeply religious person myself, it has been my lifelong goal to explore ways in which religion, especially as seen in the story of Jesus, can unite rather than divide. So here is just a brief piece of that story, especially as it relates to "church" and Ellen White.

Discovering Adventism's "Classic Statements" on Inspiration

During my undergraduate days at Walla Walla College, a Seventh-day Adventist university in Washington state, one of my teachers, J. Paul Grove, not only helped me study my Bible more effectively, but also to understand how the writings of Ellen White relate to the Bible. Our Adventist forebears believed that the Holy Spirit had "inspired" Ellen White in ways which set her apart from her fellow believers in the early Advent movement. James White, Joseph Bates, and J. N. Andrews, along with a number of other good people, were all influential leaders in early Adventism. But no one ever thought of them as being "inspired" in the same way that they believed Ellen White was "inspired."

A key part of the story is that Ellen White received "visions" that she believed were from God. Were they just for her or for the whole church?

"The whole church," our forebears decided, but only after they had gone to their Bibles to find out whether such visions were "biblical." After all, from a human point of view, grown men are not likely to take counsel from a teenager, a girl of seventeen, unless they are convinced that she has a special calling from God.

Their study of the New Testament convinced them that her ministry was indeed a special gift from the Lord. From Ephesians 4 they learned about the gifts God had promised in order to help build up the body of Christ. Prophecy was one of them. Their study of 1 Corinthians 12 taught them the same truth.

Next question: How does this new gift relate to Scripture? That crucial question is still troublesome for many. In some Adventist circles, the study of the Bible can be brought to a sudden halt if someone exclaims, "But Sister White says . . ." No one wants to quarrel with a prophet.

Ellen White's own position was that her writings should never compete with the Bible. She understood her gift to be like that given to other messengers mentioned in the Bible—such as Nathan and Gad in the time of David, or Elisha and Elijah in the days of Ahab and Jezebel—who spoke for

God, but whose writings were not included in Scripture. In Ellen White's words, these messengers received counsel and instruction "in matters in no way relating to the giving of the Scriptures."[1]

I like to illustrate the difference in role by comparing the laws of College Place, the town where I live, with the U. S. Constitution. As a United States citizen living in College Place, I am bound by both. But outside of College Place, our city ordinances have no authority at all. They can illustrate how an American town functions, but they are not binding on people living in other places.

Similarly, as a Seventh-day Adventist, I have accepted the ministry of Ellen White as an "inspired" voice. But her counsel must always be tested by Scripture, just as the laws in College Place must be in harmony with the United States Constitution. And just as the laws of College Place and the U. S. Constitution are both legal codes, thus similar in nature, so messages in the Bible and the messages from Ellen White are both the result of "inspiration," but their role is different. Her writings are always under the larger umbrella of Scripture. I would also note that just as College Place laws have no authority outside of College Place, so Ellen White's counsel can never be authoritative for someone not part of my community of faith. For others, she may be interesting, even helpful, but not authoritative.

Where this "law" comparison breaks down, however, is that neither the Bible nor the writings of Ellen White can be seen simply as a binding code of laws, even though there are commands and counsels in both that believers would consider binding. This is a volatile topic, to be sure. But in my view, the diversity in both the Bible and in the writings of Ellen White make both sources more like a casebook than a codebook. We'll address that topic further in chapter 9. But the point I want to make here is that the relationship between the United States Constitution and the laws of College Place can illustrate how the authority of one is subject to the authority of the other.

Some of the best places to hear Ellen White describe how she understood her own gift, especially as it relates to Scripture, are in what I call Adventism's "classic statements" on inspiration. One of the important things that Paul Grove did for me and my classmates in our college years was to introduce us to these sources. They consist of the initial section in *Selected*

Messages, Book 1, pages 15–23, published for the first time in a readily accessible form in 1958, and the "Introduction" to *The Great Controversy,* pages v–xii. The "Introduction" first appeared in the 1888 edition and was reprinted with only minor revisions in the 1911 edition, the one currently in use. My understanding of the inspiration process has been significantly shaped by these statements. I continue to value them highly and use them in my teaching, especially in light of the ongoing debate over inspiration in Christendom. Understanding that larger debate helps us to understand what has happened in Adventism.

The Modern Crisis Over Inspiration

In the last two hundred years, especially in the Western world, Christians have struggled mightily with the question of inspiration. In the last half of the nineteenth century, biblical "criticism" erupted into a major movement on university campuses and then basically took over. The critics, many of them former believers, dissected and criticized the Bible with a vengeance. "Higher criticism" became a code word for destructive analysis of the Bible. Ellen White was aware of the dangers posed by such an approach to Scripture, and she did not hesitate to share her concern in print.[2]

Shortly after the death of Ellen White in 1915, the tension between critics and believers became so intense that it triggered what has become known as the "Fundamentalist" movement, named after a four-volume set entitled *The Fundamentals,* published in 1917.[3] The articles in this set defended orthodox Christianity from the attacks of the critics. Adventists would likely agree with most of the positions defended by *The Fundamentals.* Where we *should* have parted company with them was on the question of inspiration. But it would have been very difficult to do so given the deep fears gripping devout Christians at the time.

As I see it, the most far-reaching result of Fundamentalism has to do with its stand on inspiration, particularly its adoption of the word "inerrancy" to describe the nature of Scripture. In its strictest form, "inerrancy" means that the Bible is free from error of any kind. Some statements of inerrancy are more moderate. But the typical view is that the Bible is simply free from all errors. Comparing the four Gospels with each other or Samuel-Kings with Chronicles should have been enough to moderate that claim.

But it didn't happen. When the hounds are already pursuing the fox, the fox will run and hide. That's what devout Christians did in the 1920s and 1930s. They separated themselves from university education, began establishing Bible colleges instead, and, in general, looked on higher education with deep suspicion.

The effect of Fundamentalism on Adventism has been most unfortunate, I believe. Not only has it made it more difficult for us to be honest with Scripture, it has also resulted in many Adventists reading the writings of Ellen White as if they also were "inerrant" and applicable to all people everywhere in some absolute sense. In today's world, many of the angriest critics of the Bible grew up in Fundamentalist homes where they were not allowed to ask their questions or to admit out loud what they had already seen in the Bible. The same thing happens in Adventism, but often with greater intensity, simply because Ellen White wrote so much about so many things. Ellen White herself spoke a sobering truth that applies here: "Arbitrary words and actions stir up the worst passions of the human heart."[4] Another result of the Fundamentalist divide has had a subtle, but significant, effect on Adventism. As Ellen White's "classic statements" came to be better known in the church in the 1960s and 1970s, a new generation of Adventists was taught that we are *not* Fundamentalists. That is clear in the articles on "Fundamentalism" in all three editions of the official *Seventh-day Adventist Encyclopedia* (1966, 1976, 1996). But an older generation of Adventists was taught that we *are* Fundamentalists.[5] That has set up an unfortunate tension between generations. Actually reading Ellen White's writings could help resolve that tension.

My students still feel the results of the great Fundamentalist divide. It "feels" like one has to choose between thinking and believing, between faith and science. And the problem is widespread. Recently I heard a prominent American Evangelical scholar say that he knows of only two major North American seminaries where a proper balance is maintained between thinking and believing, affirming both wholehearted inquiry and wholehearted belief. In his view, all the other seminaries tend to fall off the fence, either on the side of human inquiry to the point where faith suffers, or on the side of faith, to the point where inquiry is restricted.[6] Since the Fundamentalist crisis, the underlying cultural assumption seems to be that "liberals" think, while "conservatives" believe. I would be deeply troubled if I thought I had to make such a choice, and I suspect Ellen White would have been troubled, too.

In actual practice, her writings have enabled me to have the best of both worlds: wholehearted belief and wholehearted inquiry. When I entered the University of Edinburgh for doctoral studies in 1972, her writings protected me from the two extremes—one that would have robbed me of the human in Scripture, the other that would have robbed me of the divine. I'll share highlights of that part of my story here.

Church, University, and Ellen White in Scotland

I didn't take my library of Ellen White books with me when we moved to Scotland. But the "classic statements" to which Paul Grove had introduced me had become embedded in my soul. When we look more closely at those statements in chapters 4 and 5, you will see how she brings together the human and the divine in ways that are both realistic and reassuring. Often, when I have found something puzzling or surprising in Scripture, I explore the matter in the writings of Ellen White and discover that she has been there before me, has seen what I have seen, and still believes. In many instances I have seen her develop a solution that actually incorporates the "problem" as part of the solution. I tend to be cautious by nature and don't readily go out on a limb by myself. But if I see Ellen White already happily perched out on the limb, I am ready to join her.

On the one hand, then, Ellen White helped preserve my "conservative" view of a personal God who is actively involved in human history and in my life. And, on the other hand, she also helped to open my eyes to a more "liberal" view of Scripture itself, enabling me to see the human side of Scripture while still knowing it to be divine as God's Word and God's message to my soul. In the "Introduction" to *The Great Controversy*, she compares this "union of the human and the divine" in Scripture to the Incarnation: "Such a union existed in the nature of Christ, who was the Son of God and the Son of man. Thus it is true of the Bible, as it was of Christ, that 'the Word was made flesh and dwelt among us' (John 1:14)."[7] I still find that comparison helpful.

At the University of Edinburgh, I studied under men who varied greatly in matters of belief. Some had actually lost their faith completely during the course of their university studies. In some cases, biblical examples were presented to students in ways that seemed designed to undermine faith. In situations like that I was grateful for the supportive influence of family, for the encouragement given by the Adventist believers in Scotland, and for the stabilizing influence of Ellen White's understanding of inspiration.

A good sociologist is likely to note that much of what we consider "reasonable" is often simply the consensus of the people around us. C. S. Lewis knew about that: "I find that mere change of scene always has a tendency to decrease my faith at first—God is less credible when I pray in a hotel bedroom than when I am in College. The society of unbelievers makes faith harder even when they are people whose opinions, on any other subject, are known to be worthless."[8]

Now C. S. Lewis wasn't a trained sociologist, but he was a thoughtful and observant Christian, recognizing how vulnerable believers can be in our secular world. Maybe we shouldn't be surprised to see that same truth reflected in Scripture itself. "Let us hold fast to the confession of our hope without wavering, for he who has promised is faithful. And let us consider how to provoke one another to love and good deeds, not neglecting to meet together as is the habit of some, but encouraging one another, and all the more as you see the Day approaching."[9]

In short, if we want to keep our faith, it is the "reasonable" thing "not to neglect to meet together," to put it in the words of Hebrews 10. That's one of the reasons why "church" can be so very important. And who knows when we might need it most?

Back to an Adventist Campus

Our stay in Scotland transformed me in a host of ways. Living outside of America and studying the Bible under men who saw things from quite a different perspective really stirred up my mind and soul. My wife, Wanda, even told me that my sermons became interesting after we went to Scotland!

But I knew that if I wanted to share my newly acquired knowledge with my church and my students, I would have to immerse myself more deeply in my Adventist heritage in order to find the right points of contact. When it fell my lot to teach Adventist history for the first time, I decided I would read through the nine volumes of Ellen White's *Testimonies for the Church*. Covering the years 1855 to 1909, the *Testimonies* consist of Ellen White's counsels to the church and to individuals. Thus, for those years, they provide a survey of Adventist history through the eyes of Ellen White.

As a devout teenager, I had attempted to dip into the *Testimonies* on a couple of occasions, but never had gotten very far. I vaguely remember simply laying them aside. But now, having decided to take the whole set seriously, my eyes were opened. As I began to read, I soon discovered why I had laid the *Testimonies* aside. I could almost see the smoke curling up from volume 1. It was like reading some of the more strident parts of the Old Testament. I'll spare the details here. I can say, however, that I was amazed—but no longer afraid. And for that I am very grateful.

You see, a major factor in my decision to pursue doctoral studies in Old Testament studies had been my puzzlement over the stark contrast between the God of the Old Testament and the God of the New, between the gentle Jesus who gathered the children into His arms, and a God who commanded the death of infants; between the One who prayed for His enemies and the One who commanded that they be killed. At Sinai, even the animals were at risk if they got too close to the mountain. The teaching of the Christian church, indeed the teaching of both Testaments, is that God never changes: "I the Lord do not change."[10] And "Jesus Christ is the same yesterday and today and forever."[11] Christians believe, to be sure, that the New Testament teaches that our gentle Jesus was and is also the God of the Old Testament.[12] So how was I to put together the contrasting pictures—a God who kills babies and a God who cuddles them?

My Adventist heritage, combined with a host of things learned in Scotland, resulted in a remarkably simple model, one which seems to describe what happens not only on a global scale in terms of world history, but, in many ways, also in smaller communities of belief—Adventism, for example—and often in a single person's experience: Ellen White's, for example—and mine.

In brief, the movement from Old Testament to New Testament is the movement from an emphasis on God's power to an emphasis on His goodness; from fear, threats, and violence, to spontaneity, joy, and gentleness; from the God who kills (Sinai) to the God who dies (Golgotha).

See p. 42

But how can that happen if God does not change and is the same yesterday and today and forever? At the global level, the Adventist understanding of the great controversy between good and evil points toward an answer: Beginning in the Garden of Eden, God steps back, allowing sin to produce its "natural" fruit, a selfishness that ends in violence as demonstrated in the experiences of Cain, the Flood, and Babel. Then, starting over with Abraham—whose own family worshiped other gods[13]—God leads His people on the long path from violence back to gentleness. Through the careful use of violence, the language violent people understand best, God— yes, you heard right—God nudges them toward the gentle Jesus, God's great ideal—Jesus, who never killed anyone; who never struck anyone. Even when He cleansed the temple, He attacked the furniture, not the people.[14]

God can be gentle or tough as needed—and in both Testaments. As Paul put it to the Corinthian believers: "Am I to come to you with a stick, or with love in a spirit of gentleness?"[15] But as a basic pattern, I am prepared to argue with some passion that the move from Old Testament to New Testament is simply the move from power to goodness, from fear to joy, with Jesus the clearest revelation of all. And many of us have to follow that same path from fear to joy in our personal experience.

But one more principle is important, one that I learned from Ellen White, namely, that "God and heaven alone are infallible."[16] That means that we must never mistake anything in Scripture or in the writings of Ellen White— or in our own experience, for that matter—as a direct reflection of God Himself in His absolute purity and holiness. Everything in Scripture points toward God, but "God and heaven alone are infallible." With reference to our own personal experiences, a quote from C. S. Lewis is on the mark: "My idea of God is not a divine idea. It has to be shattered time after time. He shatters it Himself. . . . Could we not almost say that this shattering is one of the marks of His presence?"[17] *A Grief Observed*

In any event, with that fear-to-joy model firmly in place from my study of Scripture, and with my study of Scripture stabilized by the writings of Ellen White, I immersed myself in the *Testimonies* and was amazed. Because the first five volumes of the *Testimonies* simply follow chronological order (covering the years from 1855 through 1889), I saw Ellen White grow and change. I watched her traverse the Sinai-Golgotha road, step by step. I saw

"...the more we believe God hurts only to heal..." 49 = Cosmic Sadist the frown of Christ disappear and joy in the Lord break forth. It was exhilarating.

On March 21, 1979, the very day on which the new term began, I finished the last of the more than 4,800 pages in the *Testimonies*. I had taken copious notes. I was on a roll and ready to roll. If any of you reading this book were in that "History of Adventism" class, spring term, 1979, you may remember it as well as I do. It was one of the most exciting classes I have ever taught.

The short version is: The class of eighty students, spread all the way across the Adventist spectrum, came together on common ground. The devout conservatives on the right rejoiced because they sensed that God's hand was clearly leading in Ellen White's growing experience. The left-leaning liberals with their inclination to cynicism also came on board, for here was a model that allowed them to be absolutely honest with all the evidence. In that class, I glimpsed something that I sensed could work for the entire Adventist family. The dream that took on flesh and blood in that classroom has been a driving force in my life ever since. That is the experience I want for my church. And in a very real sense, that's why I'm writing this book.

Summary

To sum up, I am very grateful that God has entrusted to us the ministry of Ellen White. It would have been much more difficult for me to gain the deep love for Scripture which I now treasure if God hadn't used her to nudge me in the right direction. And I am grateful to our Adventist pioneers for sailing through heavy weather on our behalf, preserving our heritage for us. Now, if only I could find a better way to reach those who wince at my exuberance and those who are frightened by my honesty, then we would really be on to something. But the Lord is still at work. And we can still pray for good things to happen.

I want to close this chapter with one of my favorite Ellen White quotes. It's from *Testimonies to Ministers,* a book full of forceful messages, mostly written from Australia in the 1890s where the brethren had sent Sister White to get her out of their hair! It's hard to find a published source willing to put all that in print, but that seems to have been the case. Yet the brethren didn't take away her pen. So she kept on writing. And during that nine-year banishment she also helped spearhead the building of Avondale College.

Here then is the quote which reveals her vision. It is a vision that continues to inspire me:

> When people cease to depend upon people, when they make God their efficiency, then there will be more confidence manifested in one another. Our faith in God is altogether too feeble and our confidence in one another altogether too meager.[18]

---

[1] *The Great Controversy,* p. viii (1888, 1911).

[2] "Even Bible study, as too often conducted in the schools, is robbing the world of the priceless treasure of the word of God. The work of 'higher criticism' in dissecting, conjecturing, reconstructing, is destroying faith in the Bible as a divine revelation; it is robbing God's word of power to control, uplift, and inspire human lives" (*Education,* p. 227 [1903]).

[3] The original four-volume edition was published by the Bible Institute of Los Angeles in 1917. It has been reprinted "without alteration or abridgment" by Baker Books (Grand Rapids, Mich.: 1993).

[4] *Testimonies for the Church,* vol. 6, p. 134.

[5] At the Bible Conference of 1952, Siegfried Horn, the eminent Adventist archeologist, entitled his presentation "Recent Discoveries Confirm the Bible." His concluding paragraph referred to ". . . our fundamentalist position of accepting the whole Bible as God's inspired word." See M. Thurber, ed., *Our Firm Foundation,* 2 vols. (Washington, D.C.: Review and Herald,1953), vol. 1, p. 116. In later years, Horn preferred words such as "light" and "illuminate" rather than "confirm." But the change was a subtle one, not likely to be noticed by the average believer.

[6] In his view, only Fuller Theological Seminary in Pasadena, California and Regents College in Vancouver, BC have been able to establish a proper balance between inquiring and believing.

[7] *The Great Controversy,* p. vi.

[8] C. S. Lewis, "Religion: Reality of Substitute?" *Christian Reflections* (Grand Rapids, Mich.: Eerdmans, 1967), pp. 41, 42.

[9] Hebrews 10:23–25.

[10] Malachi 3:6.

[11] Hebrews 13:8.

[12] Cf. John 1:1–3, 14; 8:58; 20:28.

[13] Joshua 24:2.

[14] An observation by Reynolds Price, *Three Gospels* (New York: Simon & Schuster, 1996), pp. 42, 43.

[15] 1 Corinthians 4:21.

[16] *The Review and Herald,* July 26, 1892, cited in *Selected Messages,* Book 1, p. 37 (1958).

[17] C. S. Lewis, *A Grief Observed* (New York: HarperCollins, 2001 [1961]), p. 66 [= ch. 4, para. 15].

[18] *Testimonies to Ministers,* p. 214 (gender accurate).

CHAPTER 4

Adventism's Classic Statements on Inspiration: An Introduction

In the previous chapter, I mentioned how Ellen White's "classic statements" on inspiration[1] have played a significant role in my experience. In my college years, they opened my eyes to the study of Scripture; during my doctoral studies, they provided stability; and now they offer a valuable resource for my teaching ministry.

The "Introduction" to *The Great Controversy* has been around for a long time, ever since 1888. But *Selected Messages,* Book 1, containing Ellen White manuscripts from 1886 and 1888, was not published until 1958. Even though the "Introduction" to *The Great Controversy* says what needs to be said, it didn't seem to make much difference in the church until the material in *Selected Messages,* Book 1 was also available as a companion. For my part, I have been grateful that my college teacher, J. Paul Grove, was already using both sources in my college years (1961–1965) even though *Selected Messages,* Book 1 had been published only in 1958.

The Importance of "Social Support"

The phrase "social support" is used by sociologists to describe how a particular community provides support to those ideas it considers important and excludes those which it considers dangerous. If a religious community is closed to the possibility of new ideas, it may wither and simply become irrelevant. If it is open to any and all ideas, it may fragment and lose its focus. A healthy community needs to strike a balance between the two. Typically one thinks of "liberal" communities as being more open, and "conservative" ones as being more closed. That's generally true, I believe. Still, it is possible for a very "liberal" community to be just as closed as a very "conservative" one; it will simply exclude different things than the "conservative" one does.

Adventism, by anyone's assessment, would be considered a "conservative" community. I'm quite happy to be conservative in the sense of believing in a personal God who is active in human affairs. Remarkably, however, every time Ellen White actually used the word "conservative," she used it negatively, referring to an impulse that needed to be corrected. And that was the way she used it in the aftermath of the pivotal 1888 "righteousness by faith" General Conference session. She was concerned that the church might be rejecting the very message it needed to hear. These are her comments:

> Peter exhorts his brethren to "grow in grace and in the knowledge of our Lord and Saviour Jesus Christ" [2 Pet. 3:18]. Whenever the people of God are growing in grace, they will be constantly obtaining a clearer understanding of His word. They will discern new light and beauty in its sacred truths. This has been true in the history of the church in all ages, and thus it will continue to the end. But as real spiritual life declines, it has ever been the tendency to cease to advance in the knowledge of the truth. Men rest satisfied with the light already received from God's word and discourage any further investigation of the Scriptures. They become conservative and seek to avoid discussion.
>
> The fact that there is no controversy or agitation among God's people should not be regarded as conclusive evidence that they are holding fast to sound doctrine. There is reason to fear that they may not be clearly discriminating between truth and error. When no new questions are started by investigation of the Scriptures, when no difference of opinion arises which will set men to searching the Bible for themselves to make sure that they have the truth, there will be many now, as in ancient times, who will hold to tradition and worship they know not what.[2] 1889

At this point, I want to be quite upfront with those who may feel that I am relying on Ellen White for my position rather than on the Bible. That's not the case at all. What she did for me was to give me "permission" to see what I had already seen. Since the Adventism of my youth was still largely enmeshed in Fundamentalism—and still is, in some ways—the things I had seen in Scripture could not really be discussed or even mentioned in many Adventist circles.

Groups, you see, can give us permission to say certain things and prevent us from saying others. You don't walk into a crowd of rationalists and talk about all the miracles the Lord has done in your life. Neither would you jump up in a Fundamentalist crowd and announce that you had found a contradiction in the Bible. Similarly, you don't read from the NIV in a King-James-Version-only church.

A story in Ari Goldman's *The Search for God at Harvard* illustrates the point. Goldman, the first Sabbath-keeping Orthodox Jew to serve as a reporter for the *New York Times,* eventually became its religion editor and was sponsored by the *Times* for a year at Harvard Divinity School. His book is full of anecdotes about Sabbath keeping and secularization, a very good read for Adventists. Goldman describes what happened in a class at the Divinity School when the question came up as to whether or not there was life after death. Fran, Goldman's friend and a devout Christian Scientist, was in the class. This is Goldman's report—and comment—on what happened:

> Fran, who had read the Bible from the time she was a small child, raised her hand confidently and said, "There is proof from John, chapter 11, where Jesus raises Lazarus from the dead." There were audible snickers in the room. In certain academic circles, especially at Harvard Divinity School, the Bible can be picked apart, examined, debated, and condemned, but never, never accepted at face value as historic fact.
>
> When the snickers died down, the discussion continued as if Fran's suggestion that the Bible is history had simply not been made. It was apparently too outrageous even to contemplate. "I was shocked, hurt and offended," Fran said of the response.[3]

That's what happens in "liberal" circles. But exactly the same kind of reaction can happen in "conservative" circles, just at the opposite end of the spectrum: "If you find one error in the Bible, you can toss the whole thing out." Or, "The Bible says it, I believe it, that settles it." Where such slogans rule, you don't ask your question. In my case, Ellen White's "classic statements" gave me permission to see what I had seen, to ask my questions, and even to talk about it. That was terribly important for me.

Meeting the Needs of Different Minds

A caution needs to be mentioned here, namely, that human minds are so different that what may be helpful for one person could be destructive to another. In fact, the first two manuscripts at the beginning of the "classic statement" in *Selected Messages,* Book 1, illustrate that point in a subtle way—though not very subtle at all once one's eyes are opened to the differences.

After I had already used the statements in my classes for a number of years, a student brought to my attention the difference in tone between the first manuscript and the second one.[4] Ellen White's comments in the first manuscript are firm, almost dogmatic, emphasizing the *divine* aspect of Scripture. She seems to be warning someone who is shaky on the question of divine inspiration, or reassuring someone who is frightened that the Bible might collapse. Here is a sampling of her strong statements in this first manuscript:

"No one can improve the Bible by suggesting what the Lord meant to say or ought to have said."

"I take the Bible just as it is, as the Inspired Word. I believe its utterances in an entire Bible."

"Men arise who think they find something to criticize in God's Word. . . . These men are, many of them, smart men, learned men, they have eloquence and talent, the whole lifework [of whom] is to unsettle minds in regard to the inspiration of the Scriptures."

"Brethren, let not a mind or hand be engaged in criticizing the Bible."

"Men should let God take care of His own Book, His living oracles, as He has done for ages."

"Brethren, cling to your Bible, as it reads, and stop your criticisms in regard to its validity, and obey the Word, and not one of you will be lost."

In the second manuscript, Ellen White is more open, speaking of diversity and variation in the *human* aspect of Scripture. She seems to be encouraging the honest soul who needs to explore and ask questions. Note the more open tone in these lines:

"Human minds vary. . . . It is difficult for one mind to give to one of a different temperament, education, and habits of thought by language exactly the same idea as that which is clear and distinct in his own mind."

"The writers of the Bible had to express their ideas in human language. It was written by human men."

"There is not always perfect order or apparent unity in the Scriptures."

"Everything that is human is imperfect."

"The Bible is written by inspired men, but it is not God's mode of thought and expression. It is that of humanity. God as a writer, is not represented. Men will often say such an expression is not like God. But God has not put Himself in words, in logic, in rhetoric, on trial in the Bible."

"It is not the words of the Bible that are inspired, but the men that were inspired."

Given these dramatically different emphases, it might be well to tap into one of Ellen White's "diversity" quotes to show how practical this all is. Parents will deal with a frightened child in one way and an overconfident child in quite another way. Shouldn't we expect God (and His messengers) to do the same when He needs to speak to us? Note how Ellen White draws a parallel between the differences in human minds today and the differences among the Bible writers. It is an argument that is seldom heard, but one that is very important for the life of the church:

> In our schools the work of teaching the Scriptures to the youth is not to be left wholly with one teacher for a long series of years. . . . Different teachers should have a part in the work, even though they may not all have so full an understanding of the Scriptures. . . .
>
> Why do we need a Matthew, a Mark, a Luke, a John, a Paul, and all the writers who have borne testimony in regard to the life and ministry of the Saviour?. . . It is because the minds of men differ. Not all comprehend things in exactly the same way. Certain truths appeal much more strongly to the minds of some than of others. . . .
>
> The whole truth is presented more clearly by several than by one. The Gospels differ, but the records of all blend in one harmonious whole.
>
> So today the Lord does not impress all minds in the same way. Often through unusual experiences, under special circumstances, He gives to some Bible students views of truth that others do not grasp. It is possible for the most learned teacher to fall far short of teaching all that should be taught.[5] 1913

An Example: The Use of Human Sources in Inspired Writings

When one is dealing with the delicate blend of the divine and the human in Scripture, one of the most revealing—and potentially most troubling—features involves the use of merely "human" sources in the Bible. In my library, I have a small cluster of "angry" books that show how faulty ideas about the Bible can lead to total loss of faith, both in Scripture and in God. It is the *source* of those faulty ideas that really intrigues me.

One of these angry books is titled *Deceptions and Myths of the Bible,* by Lloyd M. Graham.[6] Published initially in 1975, it was reissued in 1995 and advertised by Barnes and Noble. I was especially interested in the words on the cover: "Lloyd M. Graham writes that the Bible is not 'the word of God' but a steal from pagan sources." And it goes downhill from there. But the back cover is even more revealing:

In Lloyd Graham's study, he claims his uncovering these deceptions and myths will help everyone acquire sufficient enlightenment and knowledge to discover what is false. Mr. Graham believes it is time this scriptural tyranny was broken so that we may devote our time to man instead of God and to civilizing ourselves instead of saving our souls that were never lost.

Three things are worth noting about this book, and I want to deal with them clearly and pointedly. As I see it, they help us understand the value of Ellen White's classic statements.

1. Merely "human" sources. According to the front cover of his book, Graham believes that anything called "the word of God" should not come from any human source, but directly from God. Apparently, when he discovered—maybe unexpectedly some dark night—that the Bible writers did use human sources, he concluded not only that the Bible was not the "word of God," but also that there was no God. From what I have seen, that kind of anger is almost always a reaction to strong rhetoric such as: "The Bible says it, I believe it, that settles it."

2. Love for humanity, but not for God. If we take his back cover seriously, Graham is not some violent terrorist intent on destroying the world, but a man who still wants us to "devote our time to man" and "to civilizing ourselves." Helping human beings is fine; he just doesn't want anything to do with God or with salvation. In a sense, Graham still sees some light in Jesus' second command—love your neighbor as yourself—but absolutely no value in the first—love God with all your heart. Nor could he have grasped Ellen White's view that "love to man is the earthward manifestation of the love of God," a position which integrates the two commands into a single harmonious whole.[7]

Conservatives, at the far end of the spectrum, seek only to serve God. They ignore their fellow humans in their eagerness to be faithful to God. Conversely, liberals, at the other end of the spectrum, rule out God and seek to serve only humanity. As we will note later on, Ellen White herself moved from a more conservative perspective to one which put the divine and human in perfect balance—serving God through serving our fellow human beings. With that model, one doesn't have to worry about being liberal or conservative. One already has the best of both worlds.

Would you rather have Ellen White or Lloyd Graham for a neighbor? Not just incidentally, I know some people who are so angry at Ellen White that they just might opt for Graham. But their anger against Ellen White is just a slightly revised version of Graham's anger against the Bible and God. I believe the cause is the same. I quote again—as I did in the last chapter, and will likely quote again—Ellen White's line about the effect of authoritarian words and actions: "Arbitrary words and actions stir up the worst passions of the human heart."[8]

In that same connection, here is another quotation of Ellen White's which I use often. It links skepticism with "errors" in theology. Though she is speaking primarily about the traditional doctrine of an eternally burning hell—our topic in chapter 6—I believe the principle can be applied much more broadly:

> The errors of popular theology have driven many a soul to skepticism who might otherwise have been a believer in the Scriptures. It is impossible for him to accept doctrines which outrage his sense of justice, mercy, and benevolence; and since these are represented as the teaching of the Bible, he refuses to receive it as the word of God.[9]

Personally, I doubt if Graham's anger will help us much in "civilizing ourselves." He is far too optimistic about the goodness of our raw human nature. But his angry logic can help us reason from cause to effect, and, by God's grace, find better ways of introducing Jesus to the world. The result will be joy instead of anger, hope instead of despair.

3. Spreading the anger. Since his book provided not even the tiniest scrap of information about Graham himself, my curiosity was aroused. I discovered that even the publisher has no information about him. Apparently Lloyd Graham is a pseudonym.[10] An online search yielded mostly booksellers and atheist Web sites with testimonials such as this: "Lloyd Graham, whoever he is, has made me a nonbeliever! . . . I would like to see more from this author, but there may be no need for it."

Now a question. Where did Lloyd Graham get the idea that Bible writers weren't supposed to use sources? That everything in the Bible must come directly from God if it is to be called "the Word of God"? Most likely he got it from a staunch believer who shared the slogan, "The Bible says it, I believe it, that settles it." And it is highly unlikely that the one who passed on the slogan ever checked to see what the Bible itself might reveal about an "inspired" writer's use of sources.

Even well-intentioned and otherwise helpful books can reinforce the belief that what we find in the Bible is untouched by human hands. In his popular little book on the advantages of the Bible's health rules, for example, a God-fearing physician, S. I. McMillen, cites some remarkable remedies from an Egyptian source, *Papyrus Ebers,* including worms' blood, asses' dung, the tooth of a donkey dipped in honey, to cite just a few. McMillen then distances Moses from his Egyptian culture:

> Because these divinely given medical directions were altogether different from those in the *Papyrus Ebers,* God surely was not copying from the medical authorities of the day. Would Moses, trained in the royal postgraduate universities, have enough faith to accept the divine innovations without adding some of the things he had been taught? From the record we discover that Moses had so much faith in God's regulations that he did not incorporate a single current medical misconception into the inspired instructions.[11]

The Bible's health rules certainly represent a huge step in the right direction. But, God did not choose to correct all the cultural misconceptions at once. Would we really want to grant "scientific" validity, for example, to the test of a wife's faithfulness prescribed in Numbers 5:11–31? According to these verses, a wife accused of adultery could prove her guilt or innocence by drinking holy water mixed with some dust from the tabernacle floor. In short, taking all of the Bible into account should moderate some of our bolder claims. The failure to do so can lead to the kind of angry rejection illustrated by Lloyd Graham's book.

But even if the misconception about the Bible's use of sources has been reinforced by devout believers, we still have to go back one level deeper and ask where *those* believers got it. My own conviction is that the belief that the Bible dropped from heaven, untouched by human hands, is a tragic distortion of the truth, a direct result of sin. And you know who is responsible for that. That would mean the idea goes way back.

The God actually revealed to us in Scripture is One who always veils the overwhelming splendor of His glory and His truth so that human beings are not consumed. Again, an Ellen White quote from the "classics" is to the point:

> The Lord speaks to human beings in imperfect speech, in order that the degenerate senses, the dull, earthly perception, of earthly beings may comprehend His words. Thus is shown God's condescension. He meets fallen human beings where they are.[12]

What happened—and happens still, I believe—is that sin goes to work on our diseased minds, tempting us to imagine that God is so angry at us and our sin that He wants to destroy us. Thus the supposed gulf between God and humanity becomes ever wider and deeper. But that is not the picture of the patient and gracious God I find in Scripture. Let's look at some examples:

see p. 39

Adam and Eve: Genesis 3. After Adam and Eve sinned, God didn't stalk them down in anger. He simply went for His normal evening stroll in the park and missed His friends. It was Adam who was afraid, not God who was angry. To be sure, God is deeply concerned about the tragic results of sin. He does not take sin lightly. And there is plenty of divine wrath in both Testaments. But the instant, angry, outburst that sinners expect is not God's reaction at all, at least not that of the God of the Bible.

The Flood: Genesis 6. Things were bad on earth. God decided that He needed to start over again. But He gave fair warning and carefully instructed Noah how to save himself, his family, and the animals. The biblical story contrasts sharply with the Babylonian version where the gods plot secretly to get rid of humanity. Utnapishtim, the hero of the flood, escapes only because the god Ea breaks ranks with the other gods to give him a secret warning. And instead of urging him to share the warning with his neighbors, Ea tells Utnapishtim to tell them lies.[13] I'll take the God of Scripture any day.

Sodom and Gomorrah: Genesis 18. These cities were so wicked that a stranger was at risk the moment he walked through the city gates. Yes, God destroyed the cities, but first He consulted Abraham, indeed, negotiated with him. God also sent an urgent warning to Lot and his family. God's gracious character is perhaps revealed most of all in the fact that He was willing to spare the entire city if ten good people had been found there.

Sinai: Exodus 19; 20. The frightening revelation at Sinai stands out in Scripture because it is so unique. Here we see God's full power and majesty. The people were scared to death, but Scripture suggests that they rather liked it. They were deeply grateful it seems, at least briefly. And God gave them fair warning about the dangers of getting too close to His awesome power. Again and again He told Moses to warn the people, to the point that Moses almost became exasperated.

We can now ask the question: How would such a God choose to reveal Himself to humankind? Through unchanging oracles that simply drop from heaven? No. This patient God chose to veil His awesome power, giving His messages to flawed human beings, allowing them remarkable freedom. And some of them clearly chose to use sources.[14] But there are a couple of striking hints in the Bible that reveal how Israel's pagan neighbors viewed authoritative statements from on high—not from their gods, but from their kings. In both Esther and Daniel, Scripture reports the view of the Persian court that official laws cannot be revoked or changed, even when devised for evil purposes and under false pretenses.[15] Now, if the authority of their king was that inflexible, wouldn't their gods be even more so? And with gods like that, how would one dare use "sources"? To discover sources would disprove their divine origin.

In short, the idea that the Bible writers should not use sources seems to be part of a larger, demonic plot to present God in the worst possible light. Adventists could say that Lloyd Graham was right in rejecting that view of Scripture and that view of God. Maybe, if he hadn't been so angry, he could have come back to the story of Jesus and to Scripture and discovered what the Bible really says about God and how God has chosen to speak to human beings. Precisely in that connection is where I have found Ellen White's classic statements to be so helpful. They were, and are, both realistic and reassuring.

Still, we have to be incredibly careful not to destroy even misinformed faith. In my experience, when I have attempted to show people how the Bible writers used sources, they often find it troubling. But perhaps the most revealing reaction of all comes from those who are so angry with Ellen White that they are ready to do anything to dismantle her authority. Yet they often react with horror at the possibility of using the same methods on the Bible. When I attempt to address their anger by showing them the biblical material, I often hear the retort: "Don't you dare tear down my Bible to save Ellen White."

I want to tell them that, for me, it was Ellen White who helped *save* my Bible. And I would love to help them find a way to worship God in joy, without anger and without fear, especially without the fear of losing their Bible. There are enough ghastly things in our world to be afraid of without being afraid of our Bibles too.

Those who want to dismantle Ellen White's authority but preserve that of the Bible, often sense, I think, that they (and their children) are at risk from critical analysis. And rarely do I press the biblical evidence upon them lest I destroy their faith in God completely. But I see their anger directed against a *misuse* of Ellen White's writings, just as I see Lloyd Graham's anger arising from a *misuse* of the Bible. Once that anger is aroused, however, it takes much more than simple information to put things right again. We can do our homework so very carefully, but without the power of the Spirit, our efforts will be mostly in vain.

In the next chapter, we will address four specific inspiration issues, exploring them in connection with Ellen White's comments in her "classic statements."

---

[1] "Introduction" to *The Great Controversy,* pp. v–xii (1888, 1911) and *Selected Messages,* Book 1, pp. 15–23 (1958). See Appendix A for full text.

[2] *Testimonies for the Church,* vol. 5, pp. 706, 707 [1889]; also in *Gospel Workers,* pp. 297, 298 and *Counsels to Writers and Editors,* pp. 38, 39.

[3] Ari Goldman, *The Search for God at Harvard* (New York: Ballentine Books, 1992 [1991]), pp. 175, 176.

[4] The first is Manuscript 16, 1888 (*Selected Messages*, Book 1, pp. 15–18); the second is Manuscript 24, 1886 (*Selected Messages*, Book 1, pp. 19–21).

[5] *Counsels to Parents and Teachers*, pp. 432, 433 (1913).

[6] Lloyd M. Graham, *Deceptions and Myths of the Bible* (New York, N.Y.: Carol Publishing Group, 1995 [1975]).

[7] *The Desire of Ages*, p. 641 (1898).

[8] *Testimonies for the Church*, vol. 6, p. 134.

[9] *The Great Controversy*, p. 525 (1911).

[10] Angry people at both ends of the spectrum will obscure their identity and/or their credentials. At the same time that I was attempting to find out about Lloyd Graham, I was also wanting to learn more about G. A. Riplinger, author of *New Age Bible Versions* (Munroe Falls, Ohio: A. V. Publications, 1993) an angry 690-page book defending the "Authorized King James Version" and damning *all* other translations (including the NIV and the NKJV) as polluted satanic instruments. In Riplinger's case, her identity is clear (though her book nowhere identifies her gender), but her qualifications are not. The cover of her book has the following: "G. A. Riplinger has B.A., M.A., and M.F.A. degrees and has done additional postgraduate study at Harvard and Cornell Universities. As a university professor, the author taught seventeen different courses, authored six college textbooks and was selected for the Honor Society's teaching award and membership in a national Education Honorary. As one of fifty educators world-wide selected to be in an international edition of *Who's Who*, the author was invited by the President's Citizen Ambassador Program to be a representative to Russia." I was not able to glean any additional information from her Web site, through telephone, or via email. Without any evidence that she knows any biblical languages at all, she has written a 690-page book on Bible translations.

[11] S. I. McMillen, *None of These Diseases* (Old Tappan, N.J.: Fleming H. Revell, 1963), pp. 9, 10. The latest edition of McMillen's book, co-authored by his grandson, David Stern, also a physician, contains a similar statement: "Would Moses have enough faith to record the divine innovations, even if they contradicted his royal post-graduate university training? If Moses had yielded to his natural tendency to add even a little of his 'higher education,' the Bible would contain such prescriptions as 'urine of a faithful wife' or 'blood of a worm.' We might even expect him to prescribe the 'latest' animal manure concoction. But the record is clear: Moses recorded hundreds of health regulations but not a single current medical misconception." (Grand Rapids, Mich.: Baker/Revell, 2000), p. 11.

[12] *Selected Messages*, Book 1, p. 22.

[13] The Babylonian flood story is part of the great Gilgamesh Epic. The relevant section in a readable modern version (excerpts) can be found in Victor H. Matthews and Don C. Benjamin, *Old Testament Parallels: Laws and Stories from the Ancient Near East*, second ed. (Mahwah, N.J.: Paulist Press, 1997), pp. 25–28.

[14] Cf. 1 Chronicles 29:29; Luke 1:1–4.

[15] Esther 8:8; Daniel 6:12.

- KJV - Message
- SDAH - Praise
- "Walk softly in the sanctuary"
  "Clap your hands all ye people."
- No jewelry - Jewelry
- Republican - Democrat

SDAs
Bible
Attend church
Apply Bible to life
Worship
Dress
Vote

Good/Bad
re. Consv. + Lib.

CHAPTER 5

My Issues and Yours—and the "Classic Statements"

In this chapter we will address specific issues in "inspiration" in the light of Ellen White's "classic statements." In the previous chapter, I explored the question of the use of human sources in the Bible since it is troublesome for many. The same question arises in connection with the writings of Ellen White, an issue addressed in this chapter.

I don't know why, but the question of sources has not been particularly troublesome for me. That gives me the advantage of stability, but the disadvantage of not fully sensing the anguish of others. Fortunately, most of us don't struggle with all the issues all the time. That makes it possible for us to help each other when we are in need: You can help me when I'm weak; I can help you when you're weak.

In that connection, I find real encouragement in Romans 15:1, 2: "We who are strong ought to patiently bear the weaknesses of those who are not strong. We should try to please them instead of ourselves. We should think of their good and try to help them by doing what pleases them."[1]

In dealing with questions of inspiration, it is important to remember that what may be helpful for one person may be quite troubling for another. I'll use the issue of sources again to illustrate. I well remember an angry telephone call several years ago from a woman who had listened to the tapes of a seminar I had given on the topic of inspiration. The local conference had invited me to give the seminar at a church that was deeply divided over the issue. I had shared the things I had found helpful, but this woman accused me of destroying faith and told me why.

Some years before, she had heard rumors about Ellen White's use of sources. So she went to the Loma Linda University library, confirmed the rumors, and lost faith in Ellen White. But that wasn't enough. She marched right down to the University of California Riverside, enrolled in a class, "The Bible as Literature," and promptly destroyed her faith in the Bible, too, at least to a large extent. Yet she remained active in the church. Based on her own experience, she felt I was destroying faith rather than building it.

Several years later I got another call from her, expressing concern about the spiritual life of one of our students. Though she said nothing about our previous conversation, I thought I recognized her name. So I asked her. Yes, she had found her way back to faith, and she was grateful. From the nature of her call I knew she was a person of faith. I was grateful too.

Can we prevent such roller coaster rides? I believe we can do a great deal better than we have. And I'm speaking here from my own experience with the "classic statements." Ellen White was a woman of faith and experienced "inspiration" first hand. I believe we should take as much advantage of that as we possibly can.

I should warn you that if you are already angry with Ellen White and would like to see her just go away, what I say may even make you angrier, especially when I talk about her use of sources. I'm sorry about that. I would be delighted if you could take a fresh look. It might even drop the temperature of your anger. In any event, you will need to remember that I speak as a friend and in defense of a friend who has been very helpful to me. You will discover that my approach to Ellen White's authority is not at all traditional. But it is an approach that she helped me to discover through her own writings and by pointing me to Scripture.

In what follows, I address specific issues in the light of the "classic statements." The first two issues have been more important for me personally; the other two have been concerns for others. The "classic statements" touch on all four. I will describe each issue briefly and then address each one in turn, placing the key lines from the "classic statements" under each heading.

1. **Factual differences within Scripture.** Why is it that in both Testaments (Samuel-Kings and Chronicles in the Old Testament; Matthew, Mark, Luke, and John in the New), God has given us parallel accounts of the same events in which the facts differ, sometimes significantly?

2. Theological and experiential differences within Scripture. Why is there such a contrast between the God of the Old Testament and the God of the New? Between gentle Jesus and the violent God of Sinai, Achan, and Uzzah? And why does the Bible reveal such a wide variety in the experiences of His people—from the peaceful Psalm 23 to the vengeful Psalm 137?

3. Extent of the prophetic gift. Why is there such a large time gap between the manifestations of the Spirit in the New Testament and their reappearance in Adventism?

4. Inspired writers' use of sources. How can an inspired writer use sources from writers who were not inspired—without compromising the divine authority?

1. Factual Differences Within Scripture

Question: Why is it that in both Testaments (Samuel-Kings and Chronicles in the Old Testament; Matthew, Mark, Luke, and John in the New), God has given us parallel accounts of the same events in which the facts differ, sometimes significantly?

Quotes from the classics:

The Bible, with its God-given truths expressed in the language of men, presents a union of the divine and the human. Such a union existed in the nature of Christ, who was the Son of God and the Son of man. Thus it is true of the Bible, as it was of Christ, that "the Word was made flesh, and dwelt among us." John 1:14.—*The Great Controversy,* p. vi.

There is not always perfect order or apparent unity in the Scriptures. The miracles of Christ are not given in exact order, but are given just as the circumstances occurred, which called for this divine revealing of the power of Christ.—*Selected Messages,* Book 1, p. 20.

The Bible is not given to us in grand superhuman language. Jesus, in order to reach man where he is, took humanity. The Bible must be given in the language of men. Everything that is human is imperfect. Different meanings are expressed by the same word; there is not one word for each distinct idea. The Bible was given for practical purposes.—*Ibid.*

It is not the words of the Bible that are inspired, but the men that were inspired. Inspiration acts not on the man's words or his expressions but on the man himself, who, under the influence of the Holy Ghost, is imbued with thoughts. But the words receive the impress of the individual mind. The divine mind is diffused. The divine mind and will is combined with the human mind and will; thus the utterances of the man are the word of God.—*Selected Messages,* Book 1, p. 21.

The Lord gave His word in just the way He wanted it to come. He gave it through different writers, each having his own individuality, though going over the same history.—*Ibid.*

If one can absorb the spirit of the above quotations as a whole, it becomes clear that Ellen White has gently shifted the focus from mere facts to applications. And in that very connection, "if everything that is human is imperfect"[2] but still useful, then one can afford to see the differences in the recorded facts and ask why.

Several years ago a teacher in an Adventist academy described for me some of his students' reactions when he introduced them to differences in the Gospel accounts. The teacher had used the inscription on the cross (it's different in each of the Gospels) to make the point. One student responded, "Why did you show us this, anyway? We didn't want to see it." Another said, "God could have made the inscriptions the same if He'd wanted to." Yes, of course He could have. But why didn't He? That is the question that intrigues me.

Clearly, God did not want to make all four Gospels the same. He gave us four different accounts of Jesus' life. I have concluded that there is no better way for God to help us understand what is most important and what is less important. If we want the Bible writers to be free to mold their own accounts, sharing the burden of their hearts under the guidance of the Spirit, "each having his own individuality,"[3] then we cannot afford to be too worried about "contradictions."

And when one simply lets the multiple witnesses tell their stories, it is amazing how the important events stand out with clarity. One of my students once shared a wonderful illustration from his own experience, showing how that works in real life. "Not a problem," he said, when we came to the parallel passages. "Several years ago our family was mugged. But we all described the mugger so differently that the police didn't even know who [sic] to look for." The mugging was clear; the details were not. In ordinary life, we learn to live with such differences all the time. Who in their right mind would claim that there was no mugging simply because the witnesses disagreed on the details? The one thing the family knows for sure is that there was a mugging.

But for some mysterious reason, when it comes to the Bible, those gripped by the need to defend inerrancy place the Bible and themselves in a hard place. According to the inerrancy model ("If you find one error, you can throw the whole thing out!"), one would have to say there was no mugging at all because the witnesses disagreed. In short, being too worried about the facts can actually put the essential message at risk.

At a more sophisticated level, G. E. Lessing, the German literary critic (1729–1781), drew a parallel between attitudes toward the Gospel writers and attitudes toward other ancient historians: "If we are likely," he noted, "to treat Livy and Dionysius and Polybius and Tacitus so respectfully and nobly that we do not put them on the rack for a single syllable, why not also Matthew, Mark, Luke, and John?"[4]

A number of years ago I sat down with the four Gospels, intent on working out a complete chronology of Jesus' life. I soon threw up my hands in despair, sensing that it could not be done. There were just too many differences between the Gospel accounts. Given that situation, however, I am much impressed by the way C. S. Lewis describes the essence of the New Testament message. Here is his powerful, but simple, summary of the gospel story:

The earliest converts were converted by a single historical fact (the Resurrection) and a single theological doctrine (the Redemption) operating on a sense of sin which they already had—and sin, not against some new fancy-dress law produced as a novelty by a "great man," but against the old, platitudinous, universal moral law which they had been taught by their nurses and mothers. The "Gospels" come later, and were written, not to make Christians, but to edify Christians already made.[5]

Neither Lewis nor Ellen White felt the need to harmonize all the details. They could just let them fall where they may. Some details may just be window dressing, but others may prove to be very important for the author's purpose. That's why we should refuse to change anything in the Bible. We never know when we might need the very word we thought was not important.

The differences in the order of Jesus' wilderness temptations in Matthew and Luke provide a good illustration of that point. Matthew ends with Jesus and Satan on the mountain top; Luke ends with Jesus and Satan on the pinnacle of the temple. George Rice has argued that it was to make their respective messages clear that Matthew and Luke each chose a different order.[6] As Rice puts it: "The temptations in Matthew climax with the question as to who was going to rule the world. The issue is kingship! Luke . . . is concerned with release from Satan's power, so he concludes the temptations with Jesus' victory over Satan on the pinnacle of the temple."[7]

Do you see how much richness we would miss if we simply worry about getting the chronology right? Ellen White helped liberate me from all that. And I am grateful. Instead of using an all-or-nothing slogan, she points us to an incarnational model—a Bible that mysteriously blends the human and the divine—and tells us it's not the words that are inspired, but the person who was inspired. And perhaps best of all, she tells us that "The Bible was given for practical purposes."[8]

2. Theological and Experiential Differences Within Scripture

Questions: Why is there such a contrast between the God of the Old Testament and the God of the New, between gentle Jesus and the violent God of Sinai, Achan, and Uzzah? And why does the Bible reveal such a wide variety in the experiences of His people, from the peaceful Psalm 23 to the vengeful Psalm 137?

Quotes from the classics:

Written in different ages, by men who differed widely in rank and occupation, and in mental and spiritual endowments, the books of the Bible present a wide contrast in style, as well as a diversity in the nature of the subjects unfolded. Different forms of expression are employed by different writers; often the same truth is more strikingly presented by one than by another. And as several writers present a subject under varied aspects and relations, there may appear, to the superficial, careless, or prejudiced reader, to be discrepancy or contradiction, where the thoughtful, reverent student, with clearer insight, discerns the underlying harmony.—*The Great Controversy*, p. vi.

The Bible is written by inspired men, but it is not God's mode of thought and expression. It is that of humanity. God, as a writer, is not represented. Men will often say such an expression is not like God. But God has not put Himself in words, in logic, in rhetoric, on trial in the Bible. The writers of the Bible were God's penmen, not His pen. Look at the different writers.—*Selected Messages*, Book 1, p. 21.

I have actually placed two concerns under one heading here. One deals with the diverse ways God is presented in Scripture, the other with the diversity of human experience among God's messengers. Both issues raise questions of unity and diversity, and both raise questions of relative value (better/worse). That's why I've put them together under the same heading.

My own comments under this section will be brief, since a full explanation of *why* God is presented in such different ways in the Bible requires a more extensive explanation.[9] What the "classic statements" did for me was to give me permission to say out loud that the differences do exist. And in that connection, the two paragraphs above are the ones most helpful for me. If the Bible was written by men who "varied greatly . . . in mental and spiritual endowments,"[10] then I could say out loud what I had sensed in my heart about what I had seen in Scripture.

Let me be very blunt here: From a practical point of view, I needed someone to tell me that Jesus' attitude toward His enemies as reflected in His prayer on the cross, "Father, forgive them; for they do not know what they are doing"[11] represents a higher level of spiritual maturity than that of the psalmist who rails against his enemies: "Happy shall they be who take your little ones and dash them against the rock!"[12]

In my heart I just knew that Jesus' command, "Love your enemies" was a much more "Christian" approach than hating them.[13] But part of me felt guilty for thinking such thoughts about "inspired" writers, much less about saying those things out loud. It was one thing to read about David's violent acts in real life. But when God publishes violent prayers in the Bible, could I admit that Jesus' prayer was a much better example for me than those others?

So when I heard Ellen White declare that the Bible writers "differed widely . . . in mental and spiritual endowments,"[14] I was ready with my Amen! And when I also heard her say that "men will often say such an expression is not like God,"[15] saying, in effect, "They're right; that expression is not like God," I almost stood up and cheered! In my soul I knew what was true, but felt as though I would be scolded by someone if I said it out loud. Here Ellen White not only said it out loud, she put it in print and signed her name!

Now, she didn't really say, "You're right!" She was gentler than that. But what she did say means the same, "God has not put Himself in words, in logic, in rhetoric on trial in the Bible."[16] Another Amen!

But what I also learned from Ellen White was that I didn't have to throw away those parts of the Bible that represent "lower" levels of spiritual maturity. Indeed, I learned that I very much needed those prayers to help me move toward the "higher" levels. I needed to learn to be honest with my own brutal heart, to get those things out in the open so that God could begin to heal me.[17]

In Matthew 5, Jesus Himself clearly shows that it is possible to talk about "better" and "worse" and still honor both as being fully part of God's in-spired Scripture. Six times He exclaims, "You have heard . . . but I say." The comparisons are clear. But all of them fall under one powerful heading: "Do not think that I have come to abolish the Law or the Prophets; I have come not to abolish but to fulfill."[18] Jesus could not be clearer when He says that "fulfill" does not mean "abolish." Rather, it means something like "filling full" of new and deeper meaning—while still leaving the old in place to help us as we grow.

What Jesus' audience had always heard was, "Don't commit murder." Now, says Jesus, even if you are angry (murderously angry?), you will be liable to the judgment (Matthew 5:21, 22) "Oh . . ." And "Ouch . . . "

Is it easier to keep from killing or to keep from being angry? Do you see how Jesus raises the bar? But when I discover the anger in my soul, I need to get it out so that the Lord can heal it—while still keeping Jesus' beautiful ideal in place.

The problem is that we are so easily crushed by our ideals. When we fall short again and again, we struggle with the powerful temptation just to give up because the ideal seems so impossible. But if we look to Jesus, He will help us keep on keeping on. And that is so very important.

An Australian scholar, Arthur Patrick, shared some lines with me from Carl Shurz (1829–1906), a German-American politician and journalist. I find them very helpful:

> Ideals are like stars. You will not succeed in touching them with your hands. But, like the seafaring man on the desert of waters, you can choose them as your guides. And following them, you reach your destiny.

In concluding this section, I want to make brief comments under three headings, all of which deserve fuller attention (but not here), and all of which have to do with how the followers of Jesus are to live in a violent and evil world.

A. The violence of God. I am fully convinced that at the end of time, God will cleanse the earth of all evil. But I see the end-time cleansing as a sad and tragic necessity to make the universe safe and secure for all those who want to follow the law of love. I recoil from seeing God in any sense "getting even" with His enemies, the way we too often want to "get even" with ours. My conclusions are driven by my knowledge of the story of Jesus. When God destroys, He is not just "getting even." But He is God, and in the end He will restore the universe to purity.

In much of the Bible, however, God acts with violence. Even though the "theocracy" argument is the one I hear most often to justify this violence, I am becoming more and more troubled by that explanation, for it simply says a powerful God has a right to be violent simply because He is God. End of discussion.

I am prepared to argue with passion that the violence of God in the Old Testament is His radical adaptation to meet the expectations of a people turned violent through sin. The only way for a patient God to win the hearts of violent people is to use the language and methods they understand. Mt. Sinai is indeed a "revelation" in precisely that respect.

And the distortion caused by violence is very much with us today. A colleague once told me of a conversation with an Adventist believer from a third-world country. The man told him that as a result of his experience at Andrews University, he had become convinced that the men in his tribe should no longer beat their wives. Returning home, he was able, in time, to win the men over to his nonviolent ideal. But then the wives began to complain: "Why don't our husbands love us anymore? They don't beat us like they used to."

Nor are the distortions caused by violence limited to third-world countries. I know a devout Adventist woman who took on a teaching job at a county juvenile detention center.[19] Her pupils were between the ages of eleven and nineteen, and all of them had committed felonies in the county. One of the girls came up to her one day and asked rather shyly, "How often does your husband beat you?" The teacher was startled, "Why, my husband doesn't beat me at all. He loves me."

After a moment's hesitation, the girl went on, "But if your husband really loves you, he would beat you. Your parents beat you to show that they love you; your boyfriend does the same; when you join a gang, the members beat you to show you that they care; and when you get married, your husband beats you. I feel sorry for you, Mrs. C., that your husband doesn't love you."

How does God communicate love to people like that? Without gentle believers to model gentle love, God has to step back and reach the people with the only kind of language they understand: violence. In short, the violence of God in the Old Testament tells us first of all about the violent people He is trying to reach. If you want to know what God is *really* like, look to Jesus. How many people did He kill? None. How many people did He strike? None. The Gospels record only two violent miracles performed by Jesus, neither of them involving people—sending the pigs into the sea and cursing the fig tree.[20]

To be sure, Jesus told stories which spoke of judgment, even violent judgment. But those accounts point to the final judgment. Jesus was never soft on sin. But His goal was to turn violent sinners into gentle, forgiven and forgiving, saints.

B. Use of force in self-defense, in defense of others, and in national defense. My own view is that these are all practical matters which Christians must face. But I would want to urge two principles: First, the use of minimal force; and second, a Christlike attitude. And whenever possible we should be in the business of saving life, not taking it.

C. Anger. The Bible itself admonishes us, "Be angry but do not sin."[21] There would be something very wrong with a Christian who is not angered at injustice and oppression. But murderous anger is always wrong.[22] And, generally, when we ourselves are on the receiving end of injustice, it is spiritually healthier if someone else comes to our defense. Spiritually, we are on dangerous ground when we defend ourselves. It may be necessary in emergencies. But if the church is healthy, its members will come to the defense of others and allow others to defend them.

3. Extent of the Prophetic Gift

Question: Why is there such a large time gap between the manifestations of the Spirit in the New Testament and their reappearance in Adventism?

Quotes from the classics:

In harmony with the word of God, His Spirit was to continue its work throughout the period of the gospel dispensation. During the ages while the Scriptures of both the Old and the New Testament were being given, the Holy Spirit did not cease to communicate light to individual minds, apart from the revelations to be embodied in the Sacred Canon. The Bible itself relates how, through the Holy Spirit, men received warning, reproof, counsel, and instruction, in matters in no way relating to the giving of the Scriptures.

And mention is made of prophets in different ages, of whose utterances nothing is recorded. In like manner, after the close of the canon of the Scripture, the Holy Spirit was still to continue its work, to enlighten, warn, and comfort the children of God.—*The Great Controversy*, p. viii.

Scripture plainly teaches that these promises, so far from being limited to apostolic days, extend to the church of Christ in all ages. —*Ibid.*

The problem of the gap between New Testament times and the time of the Advent Movement, as far as the prophetic gift is concerned, is not really a problem. It is either a misunderstanding or simply an error. Ellen White's position was quite clear: There never was a gap, and there never will be.

The real question, then, is whether or not a community will always formally recognize the gift in the way Seventh-day Adventists have recognized Ellen White's prophetic gift. My own judgment is that such recognition is likely to be rare.

I would also note that given the Adventist understanding of the "great controversy," God's higher expectation might be for us to stand firm for Him in the absence of spectacular special gifts. In his book, *Disappointment with God*, Philip Yancey argues that in Scripture, a spike in miraculous activity generally marks a time of spiritual weakness, not a time of spiritual strength. Commenting on Israel's wilderness experience, he says: "Would a burst of miracles nourish faith? Not the kind of faith God seems interested in, evidently. The Israelites give ample proof that signs may only addict us to signs, not to God."[23] Two of my favorite C. S. Lewis quotes point in the same direction. The first is from *The Screwtape Letters*, a kind of backwards theology with truth seen through the eyes of a devil (Screwtape) who is teaching his nephew (Wormwood) how to lead the patient (a person) away from the Enemy (God). This quote is from the mouth of Screwtape:

He wants them to learn to walk and must therefore take away His hand; and if only the will to walk is really there He is pleased even with their stumbles. Do not be deceived, Wormwood. Our cause is never more in danger than when a human, no longer desiring, but still intending, to do our Enemy's will, looks round upon a universe from which every trace of Him seems to have vanished, and asks why he has been forsaken, and still obeys.[24]

My other favorite Lewis quote forms the conclusion of his essay, "The Efficacy of Prayer," one of the finest short pieces I know on petitionary prayer, originally published in *The Atlantic Monthly*, no less!

> I dare not leave out the hard saying which I once heard from an experienced Christian: "I have seen many striking answers to prayer and more than one that I thought miraculous. But they usually come at the beginning: before conversion, or soon after it. As the Christian life proceeds, they tend to be rarer. The refusals, too, are not only more frequent; they become more unmistakable, more emphatic."
>
> Does God then forsake just those who serve Him best? Well, He who served Him best of all said, near His tortured death, "Why hast thou forsaken me?" When God becomes man, that Man, of all others, is least comforted by God, at His greatest need. There is a mystery here which, even if I had the power, I might not have the courage to explore. Meanwhile, little people like you and me, if our prayers are sometimes granted, beyond all hope and probability, had better not draw hasty conclusions to our own advantage. If we were stronger, we might be less tenderly treated. If we were braver, we might be sent, with far less help, to defend far more desperate posts in the great battle.[25]

In sum, God is willing to give gifts as needed and always has been. How obvious those gifts may be to others is quite another matter. And in the light of the great conflict between good and evil, God's hopes for us are succinctly stated in the familiar words of Ellen White: He simply wants us to "stand for the right though the heavens fall."[26]

4. Inspired Writers' Use of Sources

Question: How can an inspired writer borrow from uninspired writers without compromising divine authority?

Quotes from the classics:

God has been pleased to communicate His truth to the world by human agencies, and He Himself, by His Holy Spirit, qualified men and enabled them to do this work. He guided the mind in the selection of what to speak and what to write.—*The Great Controversy,* p. vi.

The great events which have marked the progress of reform in past ages are matters of history, well known and universally acknowledged by the Protestant world; they are facts which none can gainsay. This history I have presented briefly, in accordance with the scope of the book, and the brevity which must necessarily be observed, the facts having been condensed into as little space as seemed consistent with a proper understanding of their application. In some cases where a historian has so grouped together events as to afford, in brief, a comprehensive view of the subject, or has summarized details in a convenient manner, his words have been quoted; but in some instances no specific credit has been given, since the quotations are not given for the purpose of citing that writer as authority, but because his statement affords a ready and forcible presentation of the subject. In narrating the experience and views of those carrying forward the work of reform in our own time, similar use has been made of their published works.—*Ibid.*, pp. xi, xii.

Ellen White's use of sources—without proper documentation, it is said—has been a major stumbling block for those who are inclined to reject her authority.[27] That was also a major factor in the loss of faith in the Bible in the nineteenth century when scholars discovered that the Bible wasn't as unique as it had been thought to be, but was very much in touch with ancient Near Eastern culture. Thus its authors did not hesitate to borrow from "uninspired" sources. I will not document such matters here. But in chapter 4, I did explore at some length the apparent rationale which seems to have contributed to the loss of faith, indeed the angry loss of faith.

Based on my own observations, I believe the psychology and rationale of those who reject Ellen White because of her use of sources closely parallel the experience of those who reject Scripture and God for similar reasons. In short, when—for whatever reason—"inspired" writings come to be seen and felt as oppressive, then finding "merely human" sources can eliminate the oppression. At the atheist end of the spectrum, both the authority of the oppressive sacred text and authority of the God behind it can collapse when the use of external sources is discovered. Thus the atheist is free, no longer oppressed either by the Bible or by God.

Many of Ellen White's critics have felt oppressed by her ministry, either for lifestyle reasons (she tells us what to do) or for intellectual reasons (she limits both thinking and research). Some former Adventists have moved to an atheist or agnostic position; others attempt to live in a half-way house, eliminating everything known to be from a human source, but still retaining belief in God, the Bible, and whatever they can see in her writings that did not come from human sources. When I pressed a vocal Ellen White critic to explain his zeal in uncovering Ellen White's human sources, his response was simple and revealing: "I'm free," he said. In short, anything from a human source could no longer oppress him in the name of God.

Part of the reason for this book is to provide the kind of rationale that would enable us to honestly and conscientiously appreciate Ellen White's "authority" without perceiving it as oppressive. That development will become clearer as we proceed.

Turning now to the question of sources, the first quote above contains a word which I would describe as suggestive, but not final. It was J. Paul Grove who pointed it out to me. Ellen White says that God guided the mind in the "selection" of what to speak and write. Could that imply the selection of sources? It could. But the comment is hardly a bold one and could easily be overlooked.

The next quotation is much more revealing, but would probably be most helpful against the backdrop of a discussion as to why Ellen White did not identify her sources more openly. I'll deal with that issue first.

Why Didn't Ellen White Say More About Her Use of Sources? Some Suggestions

If you are already hostile toward Ellen White, this is the point where I am most likely to lose you. But those who are neutral toward her, or positive, may find this discussion helpful.

First, I would like to note two of her quotes which have been wrongly used, I believe, to support the argument that she deliberately concealed her use of sources:

> I am just as dependent upon the Spirit of the Lord in relating or writing a vision as in having the vision. It is impossible for me to call up things which have been shown me unless the Lord brings them before me at the time that He is pleased to have me relate or write them.[28]

> Although I am as dependent upon the Spirit of the Lord in writing my views as I am in receiving them, yet the words I employ in describing what I have seen are my own, unless they be those spoken to me by an angel, which I always enclose in marks of quotation.[29]

I have always been puzzled when critics cite these particular passages as proof of a cover-up. The first one is clearly talking about divine guidance when Ellen White shares visionary material. She is *not* addressing the question of her use of human sources, though I am sure that she would claim divine guidance there, too. But, even knowing what we now know about Ellen White's use of sources, I cannot see a single word in that particular quote that should be altered in the name of honesty or disclosure.

The second quotation is likewise clear, it seems to me. She simply does not want to implicate God directly for what she writes: When she says "the words I employ in describing what I have seen are my own," she clearly means that they are her words, not God's. The human source of her own words is not the issue. Again, even knowing what we now know about Ellen White's use of sources, I cannot see a single word that should be altered in the name of honesty or disclosure.

It is true, nevertheless, that Ellen White said very little about her use of sources. The final paragraphs of the "Introduction" of *The Great Controversy* represent a notable exception. We will discuss that passage below. But first let me note four factors that have helped me explain the way she handled sources.

A. Her readers held a very conservative view of inspiration. In the modern world outside of Adventism, disclosure of the Bible writers' use of sources has not led to happy results from a believer's perspective. In some cases, faith has collapsed; in others, believers simply have ignored the evidence. Adventists were (and are) conservative Christians and are vulnerable to the evidence in the same way that other conservative Christians are. In Ellen White's day, a sudden "liberal" disclosure of her use of sources would likely have resulted in very negative results. I certainly find that a real hazard for students from a conservative background.

In 1883, a flap over the editing and republication of *Testimonies for the Church* provides a good example of the rough sledding that results from the introduction of a "liberal" idea into a "conservative" community. When the plates used to print *Testimonies for the Church* needed to be replaced, Ellen White wanted to make improvements before the books were reprinted. A formal action approving the changes and republication was passed by the 1883 General Conference and included a rationale:

> Many of these testimonies were written under the most unfavorable circumstance, the writer being too heavily pressed with anxiety and labor to devote critical thought to the grammatical perfection of the writings, and they were printed in such haste as to allow these imperfections to pass uncorrected.[30]

Along with the 1883 General Conference action, *Selected Messages,* Book 3, includes an 1884 letter from Ellen White to Uriah Smith, chair of the editing committee, urging him to get the work done. Her letter also makes it clear that she knew about the saints in Battle Creek who were opposed to the editing of *Testimonies for the Church*. "I cannot see the matter as my brethren see it," she wrote. "I think the changes will improve the book. If our enemies handle it, let them do so."[31]

The enemies did handle it. Critic and former Adventist, D. M. Canright, pointed to the revision of *Testimonies for the Church* as evidence that Ellen White could not be inspired. In his book, *Seventh-Day Adventism Renounced,* Canright estimates how many changes might be in the whole set of, based on his spot checking of several pages. His estimate: 63,720. "Fine inspiration that is!" he exclaimed.[32]

Any kind of change comes hard for conservative communities, and the change is even harder when "inspired" writings and/or long-held teachings of the church are involved. As Adventism was moving toward acceptance of a Trinitarian theology, for example, ministers at one camp meeting took a voice vote asking for a halt to presentations that favored seeing the Holy Spirit as a "Person of the Godhead."[33]

In short, given what Ellen White knew about the conservative convictions of her audience, she instinctively said very little about her use of sources.

B. Devotional writings seldom incorporate careful documentation. It is unrealistic to expect Ellen White to provide documentation when her purpose was primarily devotional. "Melting my way into the feelings of the congregation," was the way she described her work when traveling with husband James.[34]

Even today, especially today, publishers avoid documentation in published devotional material. *The Message,* for example, Eugene Peterson's highly popular contemporary language Bible (2002), includes no verse numbers at all. The same is true of *The Reader's Digest Bible* (1982), a reader-friendly version of the Bible condensed from the Revised Standard Version.

The issue with Ellen White's writings is authority, and pressing the documentation question is another way of escaping her authority, especially if one has been oppressed by it.

C. Ellen White seems to have had a remarkable memory. The search for Ellen White's sources has uncovered some extensive citations even in her diaries. In other words, she was using sources freely and casually even when there was no intent of ever seeing that material in print. Was her memory part of the story? No one can know for sure at this point. But I, for one, am intrigued by the possibility.

D. Ellen White simply was unaware of the how and the why of proper documentation. The closing lines of the "Introduction" to *The Great Con-*

troversy have a bearing here. We will look at them more closely below. What is important to note here, however, is that when the documentation problem was brought to Ellen White's attention, she was quite ready to take steps to put things right, at least that was the case with *The Great Controversy*. When the 1888 edition came under criticism for lack of documentation, Ellen White and her son, W. C., turned to W. W. Prescott for assistance. Prescott, with an M.A. from Dartmouth, was one of the best educated Adventists of the time. But the request to "improve" *The Great Controversy* resulted in a personal crisis for him. He reluctantly accepted the invitation and did the work. But at the 1919 Bible Conference he described how it had affected him, recalling a conversation with W. C. White: "Here is my difficulty," Prescott said. "I have gone over this and suggested changes that ought to be made in order to correct statements. These changes have been accepted. My personal difficulty will be to retain faith on those things that I can not deal with on that basis."[35]

How much technical expertise should one expect from a woman with a third-grade education? Not much. "Inspiration" does not mean omniscience and full knowledge of scholarly norms. And such norms don't necessarily come intuitively. To illustrate, let me cite the case of a major "error" by a highly respected academic in Adventism. Having completed his doctoral studies, he was exploring possibilities for getting his dissertation published and sent copies to three different academic publishers.

To his dismay and considerable discomfort, he learned that he had committed a major sin against scholarly practice. Because publishers pay good money to have serious manuscripts evaluated, the accepted procedure is to send a manuscript to one publisher at a time. One turns to a second publisher only after the first one has made a decision not to publish. My colleague learned the hard way about this "ethical" standard when two of the three publishers wanted to publish his book. They were firm in pointing out the error of his way, but, fortunately, also gracious. Now if a man with a Ph.D. from one of the best universities in the land can make that kind of mistake, perhaps we could allow some latitude for a woman with only three years of formal education.

To sum up, I see no evidence that Ellen White had any malicious intent in her failure to document her sources. While much of the research into her use of sources seems to be motivated by an eagerness to undermine her authority, I must admit that I am interested in her sources for quite another reason. When I see an idea taking shape in her writings—I'm thinking in particular of her developing understanding of law—I find myself wondering what she has been reading. And I find it intriguing to compare her material with her sources to see what kinds of changes she makes. But that is an issue we will address more carefully in later chapters. What we will do here is to look at her most candid statement on her use of sources, the one in "Introduction" to *The Great Controversy.*

Facts, Applications, and Sources: Light From the "Introduction" to *The Great Controversy*

As I see it, the concluding lines of the "Introduction" to *The Great Controversy* provide an excellent short course in inspiration. I will simply highlight three major points and note the implications of each.

A. The facts recorded in *The Great Controversy* did not come from vision, but from public knowledge. "The great events which have marked the progress of reform in past ages are matters of history, well known and universally acknowledged by the Protestant world; they are facts which none can gainsay."—*The Great Controversy,* p. xi.

Here I would simply ask: Can "well known and universally acknowledged facts" be wrong? Of course. American sociologist, James Loewen, points us in precisely that direction with his books *Lies my Teacher Told Me: Everything Your American History Textbook Got Wrong* and *Lies Across America: What Our Historic Sites Get Wrong.*[36] The next question is: Should a prophet correct the facts? Probably not. If the prophet corrects what "everyone knows to be true," the prophet would be rejected as false.

B. Application is more important than the raw facts. "This history I have presented briefly, in accordance with the scope of the book, and the brevity which must necessarily be observed, the facts having been condensed into as little space as seemed consistent with a proper understanding of their application."—*The Great Controversy,* pp. xi, xii.

One can teach important truths even if some of the facts are not quite right. That's true of every children's story told in church. For Ellen White, application was always the most important goal. It was relatively easy for her to shrug if someone pointed out to her that she had gotten some facts wrong. She would always put them right if she could. But she knew where the practical focus should be, namely, on application.

Her perspective is illustrated in the urgent letter she sent to Uriah Smith on the matter of revising *Testimonies for the Church*. Smith had been appointed to edit the revision as per the 1883 General Conference vote, but had been frozen into inaction by opposition from Battle Creek believers. Her letter notes that in the early years of her ministry she had sometimes withheld material from publication because her husband was ill and could not help her. "I was shown years ago," she wrote, "that we should not delay publishing the important light given me because I could not prepare the matter perfectly." She was to get the material out "in the best manner possible." Then, as she had time, she could polish it: "I was to improve everything, as far as possible bringing it to perfection, that it might be accepted by intelligent minds."

In the same letter, her comments about J. N. Andrews, the brilliant young Adventist scholar, are also revealing:

> I saw in regard to Brother Andrews' *History of the Sabbath*, that he delayed the work too long. Other erroneous works were taking the field and blocking the way, so that minds would be prejudiced by the opposing elements. I saw that thus much would be lost. After the first edition was exhausted, then he could make improvements; but he was seeking too hard to arrive at perfection. This delay was not as God would have it.

She closed her letter with these spicy words:

> I think that anything that shall go forth will be criticized, twisted, turned, and boggled, but we are to go forward with a clear conscience, doing what we can and leaving the result with God. We must not be long in delaying the work.

Now, my brethren, what do you propose to do? I do not want this work dragging along any longer. I want something done, and done now.[37]

C. Authorities were cited not as authorities, but because their words were "ready and forcible." "In some cases where a historian has so grouped together events as to afford, in brief, a comprehensive view of the subject, or has summarized details in a convenient manner, his words have been quoted; but in some instances no specific credit has been given, since the quotations are not given for the purpose of citing that writer as authority, but because his statement affords a ready and forcible presentation of the subject. In narrating the experience and views of those carrying forward the work of reform in our own time, similar use has been made of their published works."—*The Great Controversy*, p. xii.

In class once, after we had read the lines describing Ellen White's use of authorities, a student blurted out. "Why that's illegal!" True, at least by our standards. But Ellen White didn't know it was illegal. The fact that she openly described in writing her "illegal" act should be enough to exonerate her intentions.

Perhaps the most stunning sentence in this paragraph is the last one, for it tells us that large chunks of the book have simply been lifted from other authors, with or without credit. If that sentence had been taken seriously, it might have changed the course of Ellen White studies in our era. [38]

Classic Statements: A Summary

The thoughtful reader will note that in the "classic statements," Ellen White has distanced herself significantly from the kinds of positions later held by Fundamentalists. When I have used these materials for seminars in church settings, it is not unusual for someone to blurt out, "I don't see what all the fuss is about; Ellen White tells it all right there."

But if the church is to be more open and realistic, as well as reassuring, on questions of inspiration, it will take more than Ellen White's "classic statements." It will require many thoughtful Adventists to take them seriously, taking them to heart, putting them into practice, and sharing the results with the church and world. The remarkable blend of honesty and reassurance which she communicates through these statements make them a real gift to the church. I hope we can use them much more than we have.

¹ Romans 15:1, 2, personal translation based on the Contemporary English Version.

² *Selected Messages,* Book 1, p. 20.

³ *Selected Messages,* Book 1, p. 21.

⁴ Cited by H. M. Kuitert, *I Have My Doubts: How to Become a Christian Without Being a Fundamentalist* (Valley Forge, Pa.: Trinity Press, 1993), p. 279. The names cited by Lessing were all noted Greco-Roman historians: Livy, late first century B.C., extending into the first century A.D.; Dionysius, late first century B.C.; Polybius, second century B.C.; Tacitus, late first and early second century A.D.

⁵ C. S. Lewis, *The Screwtape Letters* (New York: MacMillan, 1961), p. 108 [ch. 23, para. 3].

⁶ Matthew 4 and Luke 4.

⁷ George E. Rice, *Luke, a Plagiarist?* (Mt. View, Calif.: Pacific Press, 1983), p. 36.

⁸ *Selected Messages,* Book 1, p. 20.

⁹ The differences between the Old Testament and New Testament views of God are addressed more extensively in my book, *Who's Afraid of the Old Testament God?* (Gonzalez, Fla.: Pacesetters Bible School, 2003). Chapter 2, "Behold it was very good—and then it all turned sour," deals most specifically with the contrasts between the Testaments.

¹⁰ *The Great Controversy,* p. vi.

¹¹ Luke 23:34.

¹² Psalm 137:9.

¹³ See Matthew 5:43–48.

¹⁴ *The Great Controversy,* p. vi.

¹⁵ *Selected Messages,* Book 1, p. 21.

¹⁶ *Ibid.*

¹⁷ Chapter 8, "What kind of prayers would you publish if you were God?" (the last chapter of my book, *Who's Afraid?*) addresses the question of "unworthy" prayers.

¹⁸ Matthew 5:17.

¹⁹ Donna Coffeen, member of the Walla Walla College Church.

²⁰ The pigs: Matthew 8:28–34; the fig tree: Matthew 21:18–22.

²¹ Ephesians 4:26.

²² See Matthew 5:21, 22.

²³ Philip Yancey, *Disappointment with God* (Grand Rapids, Mich.: Zondervan, 1988), p. 48.

²⁴ C. S. Lewis, *The Screwtape Letters,* p. 39 [chapter 8, paragraph 4].

²⁵ C. S. Lewis, "The Efficacy of Prayer," in *The World's Last Night and Other Essays* (San Diego, Calif.: Harcourt Brace, 1988), pp. 10, 11. Originally published in *The Atlantic Monthly,* January 1959.

²⁶ *Education,* p. 57.

²⁷ Probably the most prominent critic of Ellen White's use of sources is Walter T. Rea, a retired Adventist minister and still an active member in the Adventist Church. The most accessible of his materials is his book, *The White Lie* (1982), still available for $15.00 from M & R Publications, P. O. Box 1595, Patterson, CA 95363. Rea's criticism is directed largely at the church for not being more forthright. He is still positive about Ellen White's devotional writings, especially those on the life of Christ, such as *The Desire of Ages, Christ's Object Lessons,* and *Steps to Christ.* But he takes the position that anything borrowed or erroneous is not from God. Prophecies not fulfilled as stated, which others might consider conditional, he simply considers wrong.

²⁸ *Spiritual Gifts,* vol. 2, (1860), pp. 292, 293; cited in *Selected Messages,* Book 1, pp. 36, 37.

²⁹ *The Review and Herald,* October 8, 1867, cited in *Selected Messages,* Book 1, p. 37.

³⁰ Cited in *Selected Messages,* Book 3, (1980), p. 96.

[31] Letter 11, 1884, *Selected Messages,* Book 3, p. 97. Adventist historian George Knight has told me that Ellen White finally settled for a revision of *Testimonies for the Church* that was less thorough-going than she herself actually wanted, a concession to the conservative mood in the church.

[32] D. M. Canright, *Seventh-Day Adventism Renounced* (New York: Fleming H. Revell, 1889), p. 141.

[33] LeRoy Edwin Froom, *Movement of Destiny* (Washington, D.C.: Review and Herald, 1971), p. 266. Froom is citing R. A. Underwood (letter to Froom dated May 5, 1930), who was the one giving the presentations on the Holy Spirit as a "Person of the Godhead" when the ministers asked him to stop. Though Froom gives no explicit time reference, a date in the 1890s appears likely. Unfortunately, the correspondence cited by Froom seems to have disappeared, according to one account, destroyed at Froom's instruction in his later years.

[34] *Testimonies for the Church,* vol. 1, p. 75.

[35] "The Bible Conference of 1919," in *Spectrum* 10:1 (May 1979), pp. 54, 55.

[36] James W. Loewen, *Lies My Teacher Told Me: Everything Your American History Textbook Got Wrong* (N.Y.: New Press, 1995); *Lies Across America: What Our Historic Sites Get Wrong* (N.Y.: New Press, 1999). The back cover of Loewen's 1995 book notes: "James Loewen spent two years at the Smithsonian Institution surveying twelve leading high school textbooks of American history. What he found was an embarrassing amalgam of bland optimism, blind patriotism, and misinformation pure and simple."

[37] Ellen White to Uriah Smith, Letter 11, 1884, written from Healdsburg, California, February 19, 1884 (*Selected Messages,* Book 3, pp. 96–98).

[38] It might be said that William Peterson launched the era of critical Ellen White studies with his essay on Ellen White's use of sources in the chapter on the French Revolution in *The Great Controversy* ("A Textual and Historical Study of Ellen White's Account of the French Revolution," *Spectrum* 2:4 [Autumn 1970], pp. 57–69). Peterson's thesis was that Ellen White used poor historians poorly, implying thereby that one could thus question her "inspiration."

Ronald Graybill gave the definitive response, noting that Ellen White did not use poor historians, but simply copied her material directly from Uriah Smith ("How Did Ellen White Choose and Use Historical Sources?" *Spectrum* 4:3 [Summer 1972], pp. 49–53). Looked at from another perspective, Graybill simply confirmed the final sentence in Ellen White's own statement on her use of sources: "In narrating the experience and views of those carrying forward the work of reform in our own time, similar use has been made of their published works" (*The Great Controversy,* p. xii).

CHAPTER 6

The Scary Title

I must confess: The title I really wanted for this book was "Ellen White Escapes From Hell." But that title sharply divided both family and friends, members of my Sabbath School class, and students in my college classes. Opinions went from "best" to "worst"—and everything in between.

Actually, the college students, most of whom have read precious little in the actual writings of Ellen White, ended up being most enthusiastic about the racier version of the title. A little less than half voted for the straight stuff; about the same number urged the inclusion of the softening subtitle: "And Discovers Joy in the Lord." But about ten percent urged a gentler alternative. One girl even exclaimed in class, "Dr. T., you make it so hard for us to defend you!"

As I see it, the worst thing that could happen to a book would be for it to be ignored. But as I have reflected on this book in particular, struggled with it, and prayed about it, it has become clear to me that it would be far worse if someone who really needs the book and who could be blessed by it, were to be turned away by the wrong title. So I've chosen a gentler one, one that's not quite so much "fun," but, by God's grace, one that will do what needs to be done.

You may have already noted that what I'm getting is the idea that Ellen White escapes from the *doctrine* of hell. And indeed she did. But it didn't happen immediately, and the effects lingered on. Would it be possible to say—as reverently as possible—that you can take hell away from God, but that God still acts like hell for a while? That's close to what I'm getting at. I hope the point will come clearer as we proceed.

The reason why this chapter is number 6 and not number 1 is that I wanted you to be ready to hear the message of this chapter in a way that would enable you to be as joyful in your relationship with God as Ellen White was when its message came clear to her. The primary difference is this: As far as I can tell, it took her several decades before the mists finally and fully cleared. I'm expecting you to make sense of it in just a few minutes!

But one of the nice things about a book is that you can lay it aside. And you can come back to it when both you and the Lord know that you're ready.

I should also say here that I am very sympathetic with people who are slow on the uptake, for every morning when I look in the mirror I see such a person. I almost wince when I say this, but would you believe that I, a fourth-generation Seventh-day Adventist, with more than sixteen years as a student in Adventist schools, did not "discover" that Jesus was God in the flesh until my second year at the Seventh-day Adventist Theological Seminary, Andrews University? But that's the truth.

This is how I think it happened. I had used all the right words: "divine," "Messiah," "Son of God." But I had been so deeply imprinted with the picture of Jesus pleading His blood on my behalf that I had somehow gotten the impression that Jesus was indeed my Friend, but that God the Father somehow needed to be convinced. Finally, at seminary, I decided to face the question that haunted me: If the Father loves me, why do I need a mediator?—a question sharpened by the statement in *The Great Controversy* that we "are to stand in the sight of a holy God without a mediator."[1] In pursuing the answer to that question, I finally "heard" the message of John 14–17. In particular, I finally "heard" Jesus say: "Whoever has seen me has seen the Father."[2] If Jesus was God in the flesh, if God Himself came to planet Earth to save you and me, then He really must want me in His kingdom. Furthermore, from John 16:26, 27, I learned that the day would come when I wouldn't even need a mediator because I would know that the Father Himself loved me. Amazingly, standing "in the sight of a holy God without a mediator"[3] had been transformed from a threat into a promise.

The haunting picture of a reluctant God who needed to be convinced simply vanished. "Guess what I discovered!" I began exclaiming to my seminary colleagues, "Jesus is God!" Some already knew, and some no doubt wondered why it had taken me so long. But I suspect that there were others who still didn't know what I was talking about—probably for the same reasons that it had taken me so long to "hear" the truth. I also suspect that when Ellen White made the same discovery I had made, probably some time in the 1880s, her joy was made complete, too.

While all that is important, it really is part of another much longer story. What I want to make clear here is that most of us are rather slow on the uptake, at least some of the time. God knows all about that. He wants us to grow as fast as possible, but He is prepared to be very patient until the time is right.

And in that connection, let me slip in a quote here from *Testimonies for the Church* which I think is one of the finest calls to "patience" among God's people. It is in the context of health reform, dating from 1872. But it can be applied much more broadly. At that time, health reform was still new in Adventism. Ellen White had received the great health reform vision only in 1863. Some were slowly coming on board, but others who were already on board were eager to bring everyone along. Right now. That's why Ellen White penned these words:

> We must go no faster than we can take those with us whose consciences and intellects are convinced of the truths we advocate. We must meet the people where they are. Some of us have been many years in arriving at our present position in health reform. It is slow work to obtain a reform in diet. We have powerful appetites to meet; for the world is given to gluttony. If we should allow the people as much time as we have required to come up to the present advanced state in reform, we would be very patient with them, and allow them to advance step by step, as we have done, until their feet are firmly established upon the health reform platform. But we should be very cautious not to advance too fast, lest we be obliged to retrace our steps. In reforms we would better come one step short of the mark than to go one step beyond it. And if there is error at all, let it be on the side next to the people.[4]

I will argue with some passion that your experience, Ellen White's experience, and mine, are in one key respect very similar, namely, that we do not all grow in the same way or at the same pace. That's why the above quotation, even though it is speaking of health reform, can apply to each of us in almost every aspect of life.

But now let's visit hell, seeing it through the eyes of the conscientious, sensitive, young Ellen. The narrative below is part of her autobiography in the first volume of *Testimonies for the Church*. This particular version of her life story was written in 1885, some four years after her husband's death. The setting for this particular narrative is the early 1840s when Ellen's mother began questioning the twin doctrines of the immortality of the soul and eternally burning hell. So Ellen White is dipping back into her memory some thirty years. In the excerpt below, I have highlighted the crucial lines:

> I listened to these new ideas with an intense and painful interest. When alone with my mother, I inquired if she really believed that the soul was not immortal. Her reply was that she feared we had been in error on that subject as well as upon some others.
>
> "But, mother," said I, "do you really believe that the soul sleeps in the grave until the resurrection? Do you think that the Christian, when he dies, does not go immediately to heaven, nor the sinner to hell?"
>
> She answered: "The Bible gives us no proof that there is an eternally burning hell. If there is such a place, it should be mentioned in the Sacred Book."
>
> "Why mother!" cried I, in astonishment, "this is strange talk for you! If you believe this strange theory, do not let anyone know of it; for I fear that sinners would gather security from this belief, and never desire to seek the Lord."
>
> "If this is sound Bible truth," she replied, "instead of preventing the salvation of sinners, it will be the means of winning them to Christ. If the love of God will not induce the rebel to yield, the terrors of an eternal hell will not drive him to repentance. Besides, it does not seem a proper way to win souls to Jesus, by appealing to one of the lowest attributes of the mind, abject fear. The love of Jesus attracts; it will subdue the hardest heart."[5] 1T 39, 40 (1885)

Note that the young Ellen apparently believed that without the fires of an eternal hell to motivate them, sinners would drift away from God. These were the sentiments she expressed to her mother. But now let's listen to her memories of what went on in her own mind during her younger years as she thought about God and His role in connection with hell:

> In my mind the justice of God eclipsed His mercy and love. I had been taught to believe in an eternally burning hell, and the horrifying thought was ever before me that my sins were too great to be forgiven, and that I should be forever lost. . . .
>
> Satan was represented as eager to seize upon his prey and bear us to the lowest depths of anguish, there to exult over our sufferings in the horrors of an eternally burning hell, where, after the tortures of thousands upon thousands of years, the fiery billows would roll to the surface the writhing victims, who would shriek; "How long, O Lord, how long?" Then the answer would thunder down the abyss: "Through all eternity!" Again the molten waves would engulf the lost, carrying them down into the depths of an ever-restless sea of fire.
>
> While listening to these terrible descriptions, my imagination would be so wrought upon that the perspiration would start, and it was difficult to suppress a cry of anguish, for I seemed to already feel the pains of perdition. . . .
>
> Our heavenly Father was presented before my mind as a tyrant, who delighted in the agonies of the condemned.[6]

But now let's fast forward some forty years from her conversation with her mother and hear Ellen White's comments about hell from the book *The Great Controversy* (1888/1911). Both of these quotes are referring to the doctrine of an eternally burning hell:

> The errors of popular theology have driven many a soul to skepticism, who might otherwise have been a believer in the Scriptures. It is impossible for him to accept doctrines which outrage his sense of justice, mercy, and benevolence; and since these are

represented as the teaching of the Bible, he refuses to receive it as the word of God.[7]

> How repugnant to every emotion of love and mercy, and even to our sense of justice, is the doctrine that the wicked dead are tormented with fire and brimstone in an eternally burning hell; that for the sins of a brief earthly life they are to suffer torture as long as God shall live.[8]

What a transformation! Ellen White has snatched hell away from God and handed it back to Satan where it had come from originally. No longer fearing the loss of hell as the loss of truth, she now sees it as a demonic perversion of truth, among the doctrines that "outrage" a person's sense of "justice, mercy, and benevolence." With words like "outrage" and "repugnant," you know you're into deep passion.

In her expanded comments on the belief in an everlasting hell, Ellen White sees the doctrine as resulting in one of two possible outcomes—insanity or skepticism, the latter leading to the rejection of the Bible and of God. My sense is that Ellen White was headed for insanity if God hadn't opened her mind to the truth of soul sleep. In short, the truth brought salvation to her in the here and now, saving her from the insane asylum.

I can only glimpse from afar the anguish that must have engulfed her as she grappled with three conflicting emotions: an intense fear of eternal flames, an eagerness to be saved, yet a horror of spending an eternity in the presence of a "tyrant" who "delighted in the agonies of the condemned."[9] But in spite of all that anguish, Ellen White still remembers being fearful of giving up the doctrine of hell lest "sinners gather security" from its loss and "never desire to seek the Lord."[10]

Before we further explore Ellen White's growth, however, let's try to look at a crucial dilemma through God's eyes: How can He communicate the truth to someone—young Ellen White, for example—who believes that He must use fear in some ultimate sense in order to make the universe secure, at the same time that He is seeking to show the universe that motivating by absolute fear is a satanic distortion of the truth about a loving God?

God's Dilemma and Ours: Reaching Fearful People Where They Are

Please follow along very carefully here and think about Ellen White's counsel in 1900 to A. T. Jones, quoted earlier in chapter 2: "The Lord wants His people to follow other methods than that of condemning wrong, even though the condemnation be just."[11] Quite frankly, I can't imagine that the "early" Ellen White could have believed such a statement, much less preached it. For her it would have been too soft on sin and sinners. She might not even have been able to worship a God who would say such a thing.

But did the great God of heaven love and care for young Ellen just as much as He loved and cared for the mature Ellen? Of course. If Jesus Christ is "the same yesterday and today and forever"[12] then God never changes, for Jesus Christ was God in the flesh. The same truth flashes forth in the Old Testament: "I the LORD do not change."[13] If those statements are true—and I firmly believe they are—then the difference between the fearful early Ellen White and the joyful late Ellen White lies not in God, a God who is unchanging in His holiness, purity, and love, but in her *perception* of God.

But, you may respond, Ellen White was God's inspired messenger. How could such a change take place in an "inspired" person? The first step toward an answer is the reminder that Ellen White herself put some distance between God in His absolute purity and anything said by any inspired writer at any time: "God and heaven alone are infallible,"[14] she wrote. And addressing those who had found things in Scripture they thought unworthy of God, she said, "Men will often say such an expression is not like God. But God has not put himself in words, in logic, in rhetoric, on trial in the Bible."[15]

That means everything in Scripture will point toward God in some way, but God Himself is always above anything and everything in Scripture. In that connection, I am much attracted by the words of Hugh Williams, an Adventist minister of an earlier generation: "Don't believe anything about God that would make you think less of Him for it could not be true. You cannot believe Him to be better than He really is."[16]

For myself, I see suggestive hints in the common patterns reflected in

Scripture, in the experience of Ellen White, and in my own. The patterns can be summarized under two key words: "time" and "incarnation."

Time. Thousands of years lie between Eden and the birth of the king in Bethlehem. Why? First, following important clues in Scripture, Adventists have said that God must allow the full impact of sin to be visible to the universe. That takes time. Then, when sin had reached its greatest depths, God makes Himself more visible again, especially to Abraham and again to Moses. Now, if Jesus is God incarnate, then the God of the Old Testament will be like Jesus. That means He will be very patient. And patience takes time. "To love," wrote Paul Tournier, "is to give one's time. We never give the impression we care when we are in a hurry."[17] I suspect that applies to God as well as to human beings.

Even when God took human flesh and walked on earth, He needed lots of time. The disciples were so slow, but God gave them time.

And He gave me time, as I noted earlier in this chapter, some twenty years before an awareness of God's perfect love cast out my fear.

Maybe it's not so surprising, then, that Ellen White would also need time to move from fear to joy.

Incarnation. The crucial touchstone in all my references to time is how long it took for the truth of the Incarnation to snap clear—in biblical times, for Ellen White, for me. And I will admit that I see the Incarnation issue looming large for Ellen White because it made such a difference in my life. We will look at additional evidence for the transition and its effect in Ellen White's experience. But right here a glimpse of Adventist history is important.

Early Adventists, you see, were not Trinitarian in their theology. They did not believe that Jesus was God incarnate. Thus, for them—as it was for me in my youth—to think of Jesus as pleading His blood to the Father on our behalf suggested that Jesus is our Friend, but that the Father is not. It is Jesus' work to convince Him to be our Friend! That may be the most important reason why non-Trinitarians live quite literally in the fear of the Lord instead of in the joy of the Lord.

In the past, Adventist historians and theologians took the position that *some* of the early Adventists were non-Trinitarian, James White and Uriah Smith being the most notable non-Trinitarian Adventist leaders. Recently, however, the historians have been more candid about our early attitudes toward the Trinity. In the words of Rolf Pöhler, early Adventists "were fully agreed—in rejecting it [trinitarianism]."[18] And that position helps explain the vivid rhetoric which emerged when *The Desire of Ages* was published in 1898 with its clear affirmations of the full divinity of Christ.

Perhaps most striking is Ellen White's statement that "in Christ is life, original, unborrowed, underived."[19] The reaction of M. L. Andreasen, then a young Adventist minister, illustrates the impact of her words. He was so surprised that he decided to go directly to Ellen White at her home in Elmshaven to check out the original manuscript for himself. "I had with me a number of quotations that I wanted to see if they were in the original in her own handwriting," he said. "I remember how astonished we were when *The Desire of Ages* was first published, for it contained some things that we considered unbelievable, among others the doctrine of the Trinity which was not then generally accepted by the Adventists." Referring specifically to the statement on "life, original, unborrowed, underived," Andreasen noted: "That statement may not seem very revolutionary to you, but to us it was. We could hardly believe it. . . . I was sure Sister White had never written the passage. But now I found it in her own handwriting just as it had been published."[20]

Even as late as 1940, J. S. Washburn, a retired Adventist minister, could vividly denounce the doctrine of the Trinity, calling it "a cruel heathen monstrosity, . . . an impossible absurd invention, . . . a blasphemous burlesque, . . . a bungling, absurd, irreverent caricature."[21] Clearly, it takes some people a long time to escape from the flames. And maybe some never do. What might God say about that?

Does God Ever Use the Devil's Tools?

Asking whether God ever uses the devil's tools is being just a bit naughty, I suspect, and perhaps a bit misleading. But maybe it will help us see what we need to see to make sense out of the Bible, the writings of Ellen White, and what we know about our own experience. In response to an assignment that took the class into some "violent" Old Testament material, one of my students wrote: "I have been raised with the understanding that God is the master of all good and Satan is behind all evil." There is a sense in which I agree with him wholeheartedly. But given those good convictions, this student was troubled by Old Testament passages that gave God, not Satan, the credit for motivating wrong actions and then even punishing people for those actions (see 2 Samuel 24).

So let's come at the question this way: If I asked you simply to choose between the good and the bad in the following list, I suspect you could make the choices easily and without hesitation:

Joy—Fear
Comfort—Pain
Health—Illness
Peace—Conflict
Prosperity—Poverty
Beauty—Ugliness
Honor—Disgrace
Truth—Falsehood
Life—Death

The items on the left side win hands down: joy, comfort, health, peace, prosperity, beauty, honor, truth, life. Indeed, some of our favorite Bible passages fit seamlessly into the list. Philippians 4:8, for example: "Finally, beloved, whatever is true, whatever is honorable, whatever is just, whatever is pure, whatever is pleasing, whatever is commendable, if there is any excellence, and if there is anything worthy of praise, think about these things."

But now some harder questions: Have you ever measured your Old Testament by Philippians 4:8, wondering how much would be left? Indeed, have you measured the New Testament by that standard? I remember one Old Testament professor at the University of Edinburgh, a devout Christian, who muttered that he was going to write a book about all the "unchristian sayings" in the New Testament. He was tired of all the talk about the "superiority" of the New Testament!

Thomas Jefferson has given us a good illustration of what happens when one uses a "high" standard to judge the Bible. His "Jefferson Bible," as it has come to be known, is a slimmed down version of the Gospels consisting of just 25,000 words instead of the some 773,000 words in a full Bible. He stripped out everything that didn't "measure up." It was simple, he said. The pure words of Jesus are "as easily distinguished as diamonds in a dung-hill."[22]

The sobering truth is that most of us could easily find examples from the Bible and in real life, illustrating how God has used the items on the right side of our list for His purposes, and how the devil has used the items on the left for his. I continue to be amazed by how many people have told me—often admitting it rather sheepishly—that the most important things they have learned in life have come from the tough times.

used?
caused?

Some key quotations from Ellen White point us in that direction, I believe:

> There is not a blessing which God bestows . . . , nor a trial which he permits . . . , but Satan both can and will seize upon it to tempt, to harass and destroy the soul, if we give him the least advantage.[23]

> [People] can shape circumstances, but circumstances should not be allowed to shape [them]. We should seize upon circumstances as instruments by which to work. We are to master them, but should not permit them to master us.
>
> [People] of power are those who have been opposed, baffled, and thwarted. By calling their energies into action, the obstacles they meet prove to them positive blessings. They gain self-reliance. Conflict and perplexity call for the exercise of trust in God and for that firmness which develops power.[24]

Even when it comes to such things as truth and falsehood, the boundaries would seem to be clear and obvious—until one confronts these lines by William Blake:

> A truth that's told with bad intent
> Beats all the lies you can invent.[25]

So let us be blunt: God and Satan use the same tool chest. But how they use the tools and the purposes to which they put them represent the difference between night and day, life and death.

And what about fear? John's first letter reminds us of the ideal: "There is no fear in love, but perfect love casts out fear; for fear has to do with punishment, and whoever fears has not reached perfection in love."[26]

That's a marvelous ideal. But our problem is that we live in a troubled world where fear has a definite place. God uses it all the time to lead us toward His kingdom. As 1 John 4:18 reminds us, God's ideal is to banish fear completely. Only then, can there be pure joy. But until then, God's dilemma—and ours—is nicely captured by a paragraph from C. S. Lewis:

> Perfect love, we know, casteth out fear. But so do several others things—ignorance, alcohol, passion, presumption, and stupidity. It is very desirable that we should all advance to that perfection of love in which we shall fear no longer; but it is very undesirable, until we have reached that stage, that we should allow any inferior agent to cast out our fear.[27]

The weakness of the liberal agenda represented by Jefferson's slimmed down Bible, is that, without the tough stuff, we have no idea how God deals with people who have a long ways to go—or just a little—before they reach the ideal. The *real* Bible provides us with a host of examples, some of them not very pretty, of how God is at work in a troubled world, leading imperfect people to His kingdom.

As for the fear engendered by an eternally burning hell, Ellen White finally realized that it was a demonic perversion of a perfectly good disciplinary tool—fear, one that is very beneficial in the hands of a loving God. Satan had taken that tool and transformed it into an instrument of eternal terror. And by portraying such a tool as being in God's hands, Satan committed one of the most deadly deceptions in the cosmic conflict.

What is crucial for our story here is that if a devout person like Ellen White has been steeped in that deception, escaping from the flames won't be quick or easy. Yet when the deliverance is complete, it is a marvelous testimony to the goodness of God. And that is what we want to see.

[1] *The Great Controversy,* p. 425.

[2] John 14:9.

[3] *The Great Controversy,* p. 425.

[4] *Testimonies for the Church,* vol. 3, pp. 20, 21 (1872).

[5] *Testimonies for the Church,* vol. 1, pp. 39, 40 (1885); emphasis supplied.

[6] *Ibid.,* p. 24 (1885).

[7] *The Great Controversy,* p. 525 (1888, 1911).

[8] *Ibid.,* p. 535.

[9] *Testimonies for the Church,* vol. 1, p. 24 (1885).

[10] *Ibid.,* p. 39 (1885).

[11] *Testimonies for the Church,* vol. 6, p. 121; cf. Letter 59, 1900 (to A. T. Jones, April 18, 1900).

[12] Hebrews 13:8.

[13] Malachi 3:6.

[14] *Selected Messages,* Book 1, p. 37 (*The Review and Herald,* July 26, 1892).

[15] *Ibid.,* p. 21 (1886).

[16] Hugh W. Williams, as given to me by his daughter, Phyllis Vineyard.

[17] Paul Tournier, *Escape from Loneliness* (London: SCM, 1962 [1948]).

[18] Rolf J. Pöhler, *Continuity and Change in Adventist Teaching: A Case Study in Doctrinal Development,* Friedensauer Schriftenreihe, Band 3 (Frankfurt am Main: Peter Lang, 2000), p. 37, note #1.

[19] *The Desire of Ages,* p. 530 (1898).

[20] Cited by George Knight, *A Search for Identity* (Hagerstown, Md.: Review and Herald, 2000), pp. 116, 117 (MLA MS, November 30, 1948).

[21] J. S. Washburn, "The Trinity" (1940), cited by Gilbert M. Valentine, *The Shaping of Adventism: The Case of W. W. Prescott* (Berrien Springs, Mich.: Andrews University Press, 1992), pp. 279, 280.

[22] Thomas Jefferson, *The Jefferson Bible: The Life and Morals of Jesus of Nazareth,* "Introduction" by Douglas Lurton (New York: Henry Holt, 1995 [1904]), pp. vii, ix.

[23] *Patriarchs and Prophets,* p. 421 (1890).

[24] *The Ministry of Healing,* p. 500 (1905); gender accurate.

[25] William Blake (1757–1827), from "Auguries of Innocence," cited here from *The English Spirit: The Little Gidding Anthology of English Spirituality* (Nashville: Abingdon, 1987), p. 157.

[26] 1 John 4:18.

[27] C. S. Lewis, "The World's Last Night," in *The World's Last Night and Other Essays* (San Diego: Harcourt Brace, 1973), p. 109; originally published as "The Christian Hope—Its Meaning for Today," in *Religion in Life,* Winter, 1952.

CHAPTER 7

Violent God?—More Help From the University

In several different ways I have already pointed to a key principle in my understanding of Scripture and Ellen White, namely, that a good and gentle God, the one we see most clearly in Jesus, the one who wants to win our hearts, is willing to be violent and appeal to fear in order to win over violent people. Indeed, God *must* use violence if He is going to reach such people at all.

But that conclusion might make more sense in the light of an event that happened at the University of Edinburgh while we were in Scotland. It looms large over everything else that happened during our Scottish sojourn as the key to my understanding of the God of the Old Testament. Simply put, it is the story about Satan in the Old Testament.

A more complete discussion of the biblical passages—minus personal autobiographical details—is found in my book *Who's Afraid of the Old Testament God?*[1] But here I want to tell briefly how the pieces of the puzzle first came together for me.

The Crucial Lecture

The focus of my Ph.D. dissertation was on the "responsibility for evil" in IV Ezra, a Jewish book in the Protestant Apocrypha, dating from about A.D. 100. The book consists of a running debate over the fate of Israel, with the complaining scribe Ezra on one side and the dogmatic angel Uriel on the other. For purposes of my doctoral work, my task was to determine whether the author's view was represented by the complaining Ezra or by the dogmatic Uriel (Ezra wins, I decided.) In the process, I was also exploring the various approaches to evil in the Old Testament and in Jewish intertestamental sources, documents written during the time between the Old and New Testaments.

One day my professor called to alert me to a lecture he would be giving to the divinity students: "The Demonic Element in Yahweh." He thought it would be helpful to me in my research. He was right—but he didn't know that it would also play a key role in my personal perspectives on Scripture and in my own religious experience. But, somehow, as a result of that lecture, the pieces came together for me in a way which has enabled me to see how a good God could allow Himself to be portrayed as doing evil things in the Old Testament.

I didn't—and still don't—put the pieces together in the same way the professor did. In fact, our major assumptions remain quite different. For him, the Old Testament is strictly a human production; God is nowhere in sight. For me, God is lurking everywhere, working hand-in-hand with the human—the "incarnational" approach suggested by Ellen White.[2]

The point of his lecture was that the God of the Old Testament was a combination of a desert demon and a good God. To make that clear, he ticked off the key Old Testament stories which portray a "violent" God. I was familiar with most of them: The hardening of Pharaoh's heart,[3] the destruction of the first born in Egypt,[4] the evil spirit that rushed upon King Saul,[5] Uzzah and the "electric" ark—as the professor put it,[6] the two she-bears which mauled the forty-two boys.[7] But he also came up with some surprises, passages that I had somehow overlooked. The most startling ones for me were the Lord's threat to kill Moses on the road back to Egypt[8] and God's claim to have masterminded child sacrifice in order to horrify Israel.[9]

Also surprising (and very helpful) was the insight that only three passages in all the Old Testament actually come right out and identify Satan as a supernatural being opposed to God. And all three were either written or canonized (became fully authoritative), toward the end of the Old Testament: Job 1 and 2 (Satan identified as Job's tormenter), Zechariah 3 (Satan as the accuser of Joshua the high priest), and 1 Chronicles 21:1 (Satan as the instigator of David's census). Furthermore, some of the traditional passages that I had thought were perfectly clear, point only tantalizingly toward the presence of Satan, never mentioning him by name. According to Genesis 3:1, for example, the serpent was simply "more subtle than any other wild creature that the LORD God had made" (RSV). Not until Revelation 12:9 is the serpent explicitly identified as Satan.

9. Ezek. 20; 25, 26

But it is the story of David's census in 1 Chronicles 21 that is perhaps most significant, for it is the "later" retelling—Chronicles is the last book in the Hebrew Bible—of an "earlier" story found in 2 Samuel 24, but with notable differences, the most dramatic being the shift from God to Satan as the one who triggered the census.[10]

"Present Truth" to the Rescue

The two versions of David's census ties in with a key idea in Adventist history, one well-known among early Adventists and given specific emphasis by Ellen White, namely, the idea of "present truth." For our Adventist pioneers, the words "present truth" referred to the cutting-edge truth for the present hour, standing in tension with the "landmarks," the enduring truths from the past. Ellen White's most forceful use of the phrase was in connection with the "new" emphasis on righteousness by faith in 1888. In her view, Adventists had become so wrapped up in the law that they couldn't see Jesus. "Let the law take care of itself," she exclaimed in 1890. "We have been at work on the law until we get as dry as the hills of Gilboa, without dew or rain. Let us trust in the merits of Jesus Christ of Nazareth."[11]

That's why she spoke so forcefully about "present truth" at the 1888 General Conference session. Referring to the fresh emphasis on Christ's righteousness as presented by A. T. Jones and E. J. Waggoner, she said, "That which God gives His servants to speak today would not perhaps have been present truth twenty years ago, but it is God's message for this time."[12]

As applied to the professor's lecture, the principle of "present truth" allowed me to see the following picture: The catastrophic results of sin meant that the truth about God was becoming increasingly garbled. Pagan nations were developing polytheistic religions (religions with more than one God) to explain their world. In polytheism, evil deities typically are responsible for evil. And since evil deities are the ones who could hurt you, believers did everything they could to manipulate and control them through elaborate magic rituals.

When the true God stepped more actively into history again with Abraham, He chose to take full responsibility for evil, thus preventing the possible worship of Satan as a competing (evil) deity. And when this true God led Israel out of Egypt, one of His first tasks was to establish the conviction in the hearts of His people that their God was the only one worthy of the name and powerful enough to rule the universe.

But given Israel's immersion in a polytheistic culture, it would have been virtually impossible to bring the people to the "one-God-over-all" conviction all at once. God must first establish Israel's loyalty to Him. Let the other nations worship their gods, but Israel must worship Yahweh, and Yahweh alone (Yahweh = the LORD). Note how carefully the first of the Ten Commandments is stated: "You shall have no other gods before me."[13] There may be other gods out there, but not in Israel. Israel was to worship only Yahweh.

Recognizing this half-way house in the people's understanding about God sheds fascinating light on several Old Testament stories. On Mt. Carmel, for example, Elijah confronted Israel over the worship of the foreign god Baal, whom Jezebel had brought into Israel from Tyre when she became Ahab's wife. The prophets in Israel could almost shrug when the people of Tyre worshiped Baal; but they were horrified when he was worshiped in Israel. Elijah responded accordingly.[14]

The story of Naaman in 2 Kings 5 illustrates the same truth from another angle. A Syrian commander, Naaman had to travel to Israel if he wanted Israel's God to heal him of his leprosy. Naaman's confession after he was healed is stunning: "Now I know that there is no God in all the earth except in Israel."[15] He even asked for two mule-loads of Israel's dirt to take back with him. Why? "For your servant will no longer offer burnt offering or sacrifice to any god except the LORD."[16] If you want to worship Israel's God in Syria, you must stand or kneel on some of Israel's dirt!

But Naaman wasn't finished yet: "May the LORD pardon your servant on one count," he continued, "when my master goes into the house of Rimmon to worship there, leaning on my arm, and I bow down in the house of Rimmon, when I do bow down in the house of Rimmon, may the LORD pardon your servant on this one count."[17] Elisha's answer was probably too much for Uncle Arthur, for he never mentions it in *The Bible Story* (he also misses the two mule-loads of earth). But let this soak in: Naaman, the new enthusiastic convert to the truth of Israel's God, is asking for permission to go into the temple of Rimmon, the Syrian national god, and to bow down there on the arm of his master. What does the prophet say? "Go in peace."[18] Yes, this is the great prophet Elisha, granting Naaman permission to bow down before the god Rimmon.

Naaman is not budging an inch from his new conviction that there is "No God in all the earth except in Israel."[19] But he is concerned about how to deal with his master back home, for his master has not yet seen the light.

I am stressing this point for three reasons. First, It was probably as shocking for me to "discover" the conclusion to the Naaman story as it was for M. L. Andreasen to discover Ellen White's statement in *The Desire of Ages* (noted in the last chapter) that "in Christ is life, original, unborrowed, underived."[20] I discovered the rest of the Naaman story one day in Scotland during family worship when we were reading a "Ladybird" book, a children's Bible story, to our two girls.[21] I think (I hope?) I veiled my surprise from Karin and Krista (they were three and five at the time, as I recall). But as soon as worship was over, I went straight to my Bible to check it out. The "Ladybird" book was right. There it was, staring at me from 2 Kings 5. When I got back to my own library in the United States, I checked out Uncle Arthur and Sister White: Not there. And now, whenever anyone mentions this part of the Naaman story, I ask them when and how they discovered it. The response is often fascinating.

As I have watched this phenomenon now for many years, I am convinced that the Lord opens eyes and ears and closes them. Thus we don't see or hear things until the time is right. I've seen it in my own life, I see it in the lives of my students. Who knows how many more surprises there may be in the Bible, surprises that I have read over many times, but have never "heard"?

My second reason for highlighting this story is to emphasize again how patient God is in opening new truths to His children. Naaman was no backslidden Jew, moving away from the worship of Yahweh. He was a brand new convert, hanging on for dear life. And Elisha, God's messenger, was led by the Spirit to address Naaman's need.

The third reason is remarkably similar to the other two, but has to do specifically with Ellen White: If God was patient with Naaman (and with me), isn't He also likely to be patient with Ellen White? Just because well-intentioned and frightened people—perhaps along with some evil-minded and manipulating people—have abused her writings, should we not try to understand her as one of God's struggling saints, too? He wants all of us to grow as fast as we possibly can. But "we must go no faster than we can take those with us whose consciences and intellects are convinced of the truths we advocate. We must meet the people where they are."[22]

Returning to Sinai, we see God taking the necessary steps to nudge Israel toward the one-God conviction. Not only did he assume full responsibility for everything—and I mean everything—but He also reinforced the idea of His lordship by forbidding Israel to have anything to do with magic.[23] Practicing magic would imply that Israel's God was volatile and unreliable, a God you could manipulate. That would deny the very essence of His character. Yahweh, Israel's God, was reliable and true. He could always be trusted to do the right and the good.

All that made good sense for Israel, but does make the Old Testament more difficult for us to read, for the Old Testament writers portray the "evil" that we would typically attribute to Satan as coming directly from the hand of God. Still, within the framework of the great controversy between good and evil, the absence of Satan in the Old Testament can make very good sense to us if we understand the issues facing God and Israel at that time. Indeed, knowing about the absence of Satan in the Old Testament explains much in the Bible that we would otherwise consider puzzling if not horrifying.

As I sat listening to the conclusion of the lecture that day, the pieces of the puzzle suddenly fell into place. I almost had to hold on to my chair to keep from standing up and preaching the good news in a sermon! The professor's lecture had concluded with the line, "So there you have it: the God of the Old Testament is a combination of a good deity and a desert demon."

That was it, a benediction (so to speak), but hardly good news to take into the pulpit.

The Pieces Fall Together

By contrast, the alternative perspective which snapped clear for me that day can be summarized as follows: A gracious God assumed full responsibility for evil until Israel could learn that there was only one God worthy of the name. When the one-God conviction finally took root, God could then reveal more clearly the great struggle between good and evil and the nature of God's great opponent.

The battle comes clearest in the Gospels, and then in the rest of the New Testament. But the signs of transition are there in the Old Testament itself, in particular, the comparison between the early and late versions of the story of David's census noted above. The earlier one says God did it (2 Samuel 24), the later credits Satan (1 Chronicles 21).

The short version of all this is that the violent God of the Old Testament is really the same gracious God who reveals himself more fully in Jesus. Maybe we could even say that God was graciously violent with the Old Testament people in order to meet their expectations of violence. That was His way of starting them on the path away from violence. Ultimately, God's people would understand that God didn't just come to threaten sinners with death, but to die for them. Making that truth believable would be incredibly difficult. But when the pieces fall together, it is very good news indeed.

With that model in place in my thinking, a model which sees God leading His people from fear to joy, from an emphasis on His power to an emphasis on His goodness, it would not be many months before that model would help me make sense of Ellen White's experience, for God led her, too, from fear to joy and to a more buoyant experience in the Lord.

Why So Long?

I want to return once more to that crucial question that our stay in Scotland helped me to answer, a question that can be asked in several ways: Why didn't God just tell "the truth" in the first place? Why the seemingly endless violence and mayhem? Why didn't Jesus just come right out at the beginning and tell it like it really is? For most of us, the longer we survive in this troubled world, the more urgent such questions can become.

As noted in the last chapter, "time" is the short answer—time, with freedom to choose. At the heart of the great controversy story lies the conviction that the essence of God's goodness is His love of freedom and His desire that His creatures *choose* to love Him, won by His goodness, not frightened by His power. Such a freedom-loving God is willing to—one could even say *must*—allow rebels a chance to show their stuff, to demonstrate to the universe what the world would be like if they had their way. As the story unfolds in Scripture, the choice—love or selfishness?—begins to come clear. The climactic event that presents that choice to the universe comes at the cross. As Ellen White put it: "At the cross of Calvary, love and selfishness stood face to face. Here was their crowning manifestation."[24]

Put bluntly, we could say that Satan went so far in his rebellion that he was even willing to kill God; God went so far in seeking to win back the rebels, that He was even willing to die.

A Long Ways Down; a Slow Road Back

But the Cross is the climax. In drama, there is a build up to the climax. And that's where the rest of the Old Testament comes into play in what may seem to us to be a long, drawn-out drama. The story begins with God's good world. But soon the news turns bad. The steep downhill road is described in Genesis 3–11: Adam and Eve fall for the serpent's lies; Cain murders his brother Abel; a wicked world is washed clean by a flood; yet another wicked world is dispersed at the Tower of Babel.

After all that deadly mayhem, Genesis 12 tells how God steps more actively into human history again at the time of Abraham. But the fall had been so catastrophic that even Abraham's own family "served other gods."[25] That's how bad things were. Whatever was told to our first parents in the Garden had been thoroughly mangled and distorted by the time it got to Abraham. God has His work cut out for Him.

But if, for the sake of love's victory in the end, God was willing to allow enough time to let things get that bad, He was also willing to take enough time to patiently win His people back. A freedom-loving God will not push His creatures faster than they are able to grow. They must be *won* over; they must be able to see and to *choose* the next step toward the good.

And that's where living in Scotland opened my eyes. I had come from the American west where change is a regular feature of life and fixed traditions are rare. I found myself unprepared for the resistance to change we found in Scotland. "We don't do it that way here," was almost a standard response to anything new and different. We were guests in that fine land, and in no position to "force" change. Even small attempts at change could easily reinforce the "ugly American" image.

Suddenly it dawned on me: If I wanted to convince the Scots to change anything at all, I had to be very patient, meeting them on common ground and inching my way forward from there. Then I began applying that same principle to the Old Testament. Shouldn't a freedom-loving God be as patient with the Old Testament saints as He was with the Scots? In short, living in Scotland opened my mind to the idea of "radical divine accommodation." Another word might work better for you: "condescension," "adaptation," or "contextualization." But they all mean roughly the same: God meets people where they are. He's urgent with the good news, but must be patient if He's going to win people's hearts.

Living in Scotland convinced me that the God of the Old Testament was a very patient God, indeed, the same God we see in Jesus. He took great risks in order to reach the people where they were. But a God of love is willing to take such risks. That was good news for them, and it's good news for us.

And Now for Ellen White

To sum up with reference to Ellen White, the story about Satan's seeming absence from the Old Testament is significant for two reasons. The first one I have emphasized again and again: God's patience. However misused and abused her writings may have been—and there has been plenty of that—we will certainly fall short of the truth if we can't make room for God to be patient with Ellen White, too. I hope that does not sound condescending, and it may, especially for those who have experienced her as an absolute authority in Adventism. But if we seek to understand the Bible in the perspective of its day, shouldn't we do the same for the writings of Ellen White and look at them from the perspective of her day? If, as she said in 1888, there can be a turn-round in "present truth" in just twenty years,[26] shouldn't we be willing to take a fresh look at her experience and her writings some ninety years after her death? I think so.

Second (and this point is at least as crucial as the first for understanding Ellen White's writings and experience): Without an awareness of Satan's *apparent* absence from the Old Testament, the God of the Old Testament would appear to be anything but patient. Violent, brutal, quick with the trigger, insensitive to animal and human life—that's the picture of the God of the Old Testament if you just read it straight off the page without seeing the larger picture. Now I happen to believe, with tenacity even, that Satan was fully as alive and well in the Old Testament as he is today. But for *pastoral* reasons, God chose to keep Satan under wraps, assuming full responsibility for everything lest the people worship Satan as another deity. Yes, God was willing to be seen as violent, brutal, quick with the trigger,

.EVE?
.CAIN?
."ONLY EVIL ALL THE TIME
.SODOM?

insensitive to animal and human life, because that was what the people had come to expect from their gods. And that was where God had to start.

But if you can believe that gentle Jesus is God in the flesh, "the same yesterday and today and forever,"[27] and if you can believe that He was and is the God of the Old Testament[28] —and all that is perfectly clear in the New Testament— then we must go back to the Old Testament and look again. With careful reading, we can begin to see why God would be willing to portray Himself as the violent one and to keep Satan under cover until it was safe for the people to know more about the "great controversy" between Christ and Satan.

But Ellen White was not part of a community that believed Jesus was God in the flesh. For early Adventists, Jesus may have been kind, sweet, and gentle, but He was not God. Even with the knowledge that Jesus was and is God, the Old Testament is still heavy weather for gentle people. We can scarcely believe that God was willing to do what He did, even if it was for good *pastoral* reasons.

In short, young Ellen was a conscientious, devout, and obedient Christian. But she had grown up with the terrors of an eternally burning hell etched into her soul. And reading the Old Testament straight from the page would make it easy to believe that the God of the Old Testament would not hesitate to be in charge of such a hell. Then, as she became a young adult, though the eternal hell had disappeared, she still belonged to a community that had not yet seen the truth about the divinity of Jesus Christ.

So when we read some of her early writings, it will not be hard to recognize when she has been reading the Old Testament straight from the page— without the saving knowledge that the God who revealed Himself in Jesus Christ had veiled His gentle nature in order to reach violent people.

The laws of change—especially the necessity of gradual change if one wants change to be stable—apply to all people everywhere. We can see those laws at work in the Bible. Then we can apply them to our own experience. And we can apply them to Ellen White's experience. It may seem scary at times, but it will also be reassuring. If we're not afraid to let Jesus help us, He will guide us into all truth. He has promised.

In the next chapter, I'll give you some glimpses of the other side of our life in Scotland. I was awakening to issues of change in the Bible and observing how hard it was for the Scots to change. But on the home front, we were tussling mightily with change, too. Wanda and I had both been imprinted by our conservative Adventist upbringing with a lifestyle very much shaped by the writings of Ellen White. All that made pretty good sense in a largely Adventist community in the American west. But we were in for a cold shower when we took some of our Adventist habits to Scotland and tried to live them out there. That's all part of this story, too, as you will see.

---

[1] "Whatever Happened to Satan in the Old Testament?" Chapter 3 in *Who's Afraid of the Old Testament God?*

[2] *The Great Controversy*, p. vi: "But the Bible, with its God-given truths expressed in the language of men, presents a union of the divine and the human. Such a union existed in the nature of Christ, who was the Son of God and the Son of man. Thus it is true of the Bible, as it was of Christ, that 'the Word was made flesh, and dwelt among us.' John 1:14."

[3] Exodus 4:21; 7:3; 14:4.

[4] Exodus 11; 12.

[5] 1 Samuel 18:10.

[6] 2 Samuel 6.

[7] 2 Kings 2.

[8] Exodus 4:24.

[9] Ezekiel 20:25, 26.

[10] 2 Samuel 24:1; 1 Chronicles 21:1.

[11] Ms. 10, 1890, EGW1888 2:557.

[12] Ms. 8a, 1888, address to ministers on October 21, 1888, cited in A. V. Olson, *Thirteen Crisis Years* (Washington, D.C.: Review and Herald, 1981), p. 282; EGW 1888, 1:133.

[13] Exodus 20:3.

[14] 1 Kings 17–19. The idea that other gods were assigned to other nations is reflected in many modern translations of Deuteronomy 32:8. "When the Most High apportioned the nations, when he divided humankind, he fixed the boundaries of the people according to the number of the gods." See "Whatever Happened to Satan in the Old Testament?, chapter 3 in *Who's Afraid?*

[15] 2 Kings 5:15.

[16] 2 Kings 5:17.

[17] 2 Kings 5:18.

[18] 2 Kings 5:19.

[19] 2 Kings 5:15.

[20] *The Desire of Ages*, p. 530 (1898).

[21] Lucy Diamond, *Naaman and the Little Maid*. A Ladybird Book (Loughborough, England: Wills and Hepworth, 1959).

[22] *Testimonies for the Church*, vol. 3, p. 20 (1872).

[23] Cf. Leviticus 19:31; Isaiah 8:19.

[24] *The Desire of Ages*, p. 57.

[25] Joshua 24:2.

[26] Ms. 8a, 1888, Olson, p. 282; EGW 1888, 1:133.

[27] Hebrews 13:8.

[28] Cf. John 8:58.

CHAPTER 8

Taking Ellen White to Scotland

When we went to Scotland in 1972, living there for two and a half years, I didn't take my Ellen White books with me. Instead, I took them along in my body, soul, and mind, where they had been etched from childhood.

That will make sense only for some Adventists. Just days ago I talked with a devout Adventist who is now a conference administrator in our part of the world. Even though we had grown up in the same valley and attended the same church school, his Adventist experience was quite different from mine. His family belonged to an Adventist Church in which the members were not so deeply imprinted by Ellen White's influence. He told me that he didn't tumble to the fact that vegetarianism was important for Adventists until he went away to an Adventist boarding academy. I was amazed.

So this chapter will be important for understanding my Adventist experience and why I feel so keenly about being honest and open with Scripture and with the writings of Ellen White. If you picture Ellen White as rigid and legalistic, this chapter may be of some interest. But it will depend on whether you are reflecting your own personal experience or one that you picked up second hand. And if you have been deeply imprinted with a distorted view of Ellen White, this chapter and this book may be too little too late—or too much, too early. There is much that we must leave in God's hands. But I pray that my experience will be helpful to some and a blessing to the church as a whole. So here is my story. Though it ends up in Scotland, the story of my earlier years will help you understand what happened when we got there.

Discovering Ellen White

Actually, I didn't have to do any work at all to discover Ellen White. She was already there when I was born. I'm a fourth-generation Adventist on both sides; our life as a family was shaped by her counsel. Diet? Vegetarian (but not vegan), no caffeine, nothing between meals. Recreation and entertainment? No novels, no movies or theater, no TV at home, sporting events viewed with suspicion. Education? Church school.

1. The Early Years: God's Hand

To use Adventist jargon, my first memories of life come from "the mission field." A financial sponsor backed out on my dad just as he was setting his sights on the study of medicine at the College of Medical Evangelists, now Loma Linda University. So my parents accepted a three-year mission term at the Adventist college in Medellin, Colombia. Since I was only a year old when we arrived and four years old when we left, my memories are limited. But three stories I do remember, mostly from hearing my mother tell them.

The first one is not a story she told in public, and not often even to me. Still, it shaped my life. My mother told me that while we were in Colombia, I contracted the potentially deadly tropical disease, trench mouth. With a high fever and a throat swollen almost completely shut, I was at death's door. But the church had special prayer, and the tide turned.

The second story is one I "remember" only because I heard my mother tell it many times to church groups. We were flying back to Medellin from a vacation trip in Bogota when the weather turned sour. Our DC3 had no place to land. Over dense tropical forests and rampaging rivers, the captain took plane and passengers on a terror-filled search, scouring the rugged terrain for any kind of a landing place. Finally, through the torrential downpour, he spotted a sandy spit in the middle of a turgid tropical river. With fuel virtually gone, the captain skillfully touched the plane down on that tiny piece of land; the props bit into the sand at just the right time; the plane came to a full stop. Everyone was safe. By the time rescuers arrived in rafts from a near-by mining camp, the sandy spit was gone, completely submerged under the raging river waters.

The third story is one I think I remember myself, at least bits and pieces of it, for I was old enough to remember the murderous shouts from our next door neighbor, Señor Restrepo, filtering into my bedroom night after night. My mother tells me I did some screaming of my own from the nightmares triggered by our neighbor's angry taunts.

The college, you see, needed water and had drilled a new well. But Señor Restrepo, the wealthy rancher who lived next to the college—and no friend of Adventists—claimed we were stealing his water. As litigation inched its way through the courts, the judge granted the college permission to run the well for a brief period during the middle of the night.

But someone had to go and turn on the pump.

The job fell on a young ministerial student, Climico Joya. Each night, as he went to do his duty, Señor Restrepo was lurking in the bushes with his gun, threatening to shoot anyone who dared come near the well. "But each night," I can hear my mother say, "the angel of the Lord put his hand over Climico Joya. Suddenly the electric motor would be purring; the pump was running. But Señor Restrepo never saw anyone."

Night after night, the drama was repeated. Night after night, Climico Joya would turn on the pump, and Señor Restrepo would rant and rave because he never saw him do it. His curses began to increase in volume and intensity. Then one day he announced to anyone who would listen that he would poison the well and kill the Adventists. I can remember my mother telling how she would turn on the water at the kitchen sink in the morning, wondering if we would still be alive when evening came.

He bought the poison. We know that, because his wife gave it to him by mistake one day when he asked for a drink. "You've poisoned me!" he screamed, sensing immediately what had happened. "Call the *Adventistas;* Call the *Adventistas!*"

It was Climico Joya who came, lurching along as fast as he dared in the decrepit old college van. He rushed Señor Restrepo to the hospital. But it was too late. And the water crisis at the college was over.

Those stories have left their mark.

2. Early Imprinting: People, Food, Books

We returned to Loma Linda in the late 1940s so that my father could begin the study of medicine. Two lifestyle memories linger from our years in Loma Linda. One day I ate an apple between meals. I don't remember reprimands or punishment, but I remember the apple. I might note that very few of the current generation of Adventist students have even heard of

Ellen White's vivid statement, "You should never let a morsel pass your lips between your regular meals."[1]

The other lifestyle memory is a serious one, but now comes packaged with a touch of humor. One day (without warning), soy milk appeared on our table at meal time. This was 1950s soy milk, two-thirds foam, a ghastly flavor, an insult to the perfectly innocent soy bean. The "milk" was briefly on our table—then was gone.

Now the touch of humor. Early in my planning for this book, I intended to dedicate it to my parents, for even though ours was a conservative home, their "reasonable" attitude toward the writings of Ellen White kept my rebel spirit in check, thus leaving the way open for me to appreciate her for myself. I am grateful for that reasonableness.

In any event, I had planned a playful dedicatory note, probably too playful for those who take such matters seriously. So I was torn: use it or not use it? But one day when my parents were visiting us, I couldn't resist the temptation to share it. Here is the original version in all its glory:

> Dedicated to my parents, George and Lola Thompson, who believed the time had come to give up dairy products.[2] But a brief exposure to 1950s soy milk convinced them that the time had not come.

When I read it to them, mirth took over. And usually Dad needs time to snap out of it once laughter gets a grip on him. I had two questions for them, but had to wait until the merriment subsided. Finally my chance came:

First, "Whose idea was it?"

Mother pointed at Dad.

Second, "How long did it last?"

Dad was still mostly out of control, but finally sobered up enough to get the words out. "I don't know how long it lasted," he gasped, "all I knew was that the time hadn't come for me."

But now a sobering note. In spite of my deep immersion in Adventism, I was startled to learn some months ago that at certain self-supporting restaurants and institutions run by devout, conservative Adventists, when the workers are preparing food for the next meal and need to sample it (i.e., between meals), they won't swallow it, but spit it out. They take Ellen White very seriously indeed.

After Dad finished at Loma Linda, we settled in Clarkston, Washington, where he practiced medicine until he retired. As my parents searched for the right place to live, church school was a key criterion. That, too, suggests a moderate form of Adventism. I once compared notes with a colleague whose father was my father's contemporary at Loma Linda. His family didn't look for a church school, but for a "dark county," a place with no Adventists. My colleague, the only one of three siblings who is still part of "mainstream" Adventism, told me of having to leave home and live with relatives in order to attend church school. It was hard. From that family, one sibling moved to the secular left, another to the independent Adventist right. In our tribe, all four children remain active in mainstream Adventism. Church school or dark county? A significant choice.

My childhood memories also include a "literature route," passing out Adventist papers week after week on Sabbath afternoons. I never got to know the people on my route; I just handed them the tract at the door and went on. One by one, over a period of several weeks, most of them politely told me that I didn't need to come any more. Looking back now, I realize how isolated we were from community life, from where the people really were, in spite of my father's active involvement in many good community projects.

That sense of isolation intensified when my older sister, Georgene, and I walked by the public school kids on our way to the church school bus stop. And on Friday nights in winter, I would lie in bed, listening to the shouts and cheers coming from the high school football field where "our" team, the Clarkston Bantams, was showing its stuff.

In those early years, before I went away to boarding academy, I remember being very serious about my religious experience, even if it wasn't very "exciting." Recently I went back to my copy of *Messages to Young People* to see how it had come into my possession. Though others have found that compilation helpful, it was troubling for me because it felt like a book of rules without enough good reasons given for the rules. I was surprised to discover that I got my copy of it, not from my parents, but from my sister, a gift for my eighth-grade graduation.

A little more than a year later, my parents gave me the five volumes of the Conflict of the Ages series for my fifteenth birthday. Dad, a great lover of aphorisms and quotes, inscribed a quote on the inside front cover of each book. Of the five quotes, three are distinctly religious—two of them from Ellen White. The other two are nonreligious moral maxims—one from the Quaker statesman William Penn (1644–1718), the other from the Scottish author Thomas Carlyle (1795–1881). In other words, two nonreligious quotes from two deeply religious men.

The Carlyle quote is intriguing ("The greatest fault is to be conscious of none."), for Dad did not indicate the author. Though Carlyle was primarily a man of letters, his religious influence was significant enough to merit him an entry in *The Oxford Dictionary of the Christian Church*. The third edition (1997), says this about him: "Though he hated creeds, churches, and theologies, he had a profound belief in God and was convinced that 'the Religious Principle lies unseen in the hearts of all good men.' "[3]

Did Dad know all that? Probably not. And he certainly did not share Carlyle's dislike of organized religion. Yet there was a certain breadth to my parents' perspective. Dad loved nature, science, history, languages—in fact, almost anything in book form. We never had a TV at home while we were growing up, but maybe that's why both parents would occasionally read to us. But I don't recall them ever simply reading "Ellen White" to us. We may not have read many novels (none, actually). But we read much more than just the Bible and Ellen White. Thus my exposure to Ellen White was moderate rather than extreme.

By contrast, one of my academic colleagues grew up hearing *Testimonies for the Church* twice a day for family worship. Another colleague worked summers on a ranch during his teen years where he got a forty-five-minute dose of *Testimonies for the Church* and a half-hour prayer at the end of every hard day's work on the ranch. I can appreciate Ellen White now, in part, because I wasn't overdosed in my youth.

As noted earlier in chapter 3, I vaguely remember attempting on my own to read *Testimonies for the Church* during my teen years. But I never got far (not knowing why at that point) and soon set them aside with no particular hostility (as I recall). But it didn't take much exposure to *Messages to Young People* to trigger a hostile reaction to *that* book.[4] Twenty years later (1970s), I would return to *Testimonies for the Church* and read the volumes with high interest and much profit. That's also when I learned the importance of context. All the tedious lists of prohibitions, strung out like beads on a string in *Messages to Young People,* suddenly became understandable when I saw them in *Testimonies for the Church* with context and rationale spelled out.

On balance, however, I have concluded fairly recently that I am a rather odd duck. That's easier to say now than it was then. When I went to Upper Columbia Academy for my last two years of high school, I was lonelier than I wanted to admit. I was serious about grades and religion and not much into exuberant adolescent antics. And I was probably still suffering some culture shock because of my parents' mission experience, even though it had happened some ten years earlier. I desperately wanted to be liked, but in a teen crowd, the harder you try the worse it gets. A few years ago at a UCA alumni reunion, a second-hand quote from one of my former teachers got back to me, "He was certainly one of the most unusual teenagers we ever saw." Probably so. And maybe that's why I'm writing this book.

During my undergraduate years at Walla Walla College, I was hard-driving, still serious about my studies, and much involved in extracurricular activities—I desperately wanted to prove to the world (and to myself) that I was competent and capable. I read papers for three years for J. Paul Grove, a devout, God-fearing teacher in the School of Theology, a significant mentor. Not only did he teach me how to read the Bible, he also helped me see the significance of motive in all my "good" works. Fragile light began to illumine the evil lurking in my highly competitive, ego-driven soul.

And as I noted earlier, it was also J. Paul Grove who first introduced me to Ellen White's statements on inspiration in *Selected Messages,* Book 1, pp. 15–23. Recently I asked him how he had come across those statements so soon after they were published—*Selected Messages,* Book 1, appeared in 1958; I arrived at Walla Walla College as a freshman theology major in 1961. Paul doesn't remember how he found them. But I'm grateful he did and grateful he shared them.

In college, I also began to sense that there was something wrong with what seemed to be a popular assumption about "inspired" writings, one which is virtually a proverb in many Fundamentalist circles: "If you find one error in the Bible, you can toss the whole thing out." Adventists don't use that saying much, but the idea certainly forms the backdrop for most discussions about inspiration. I knew I wouldn't dump my friends for one "error." Why should I do that with my Bible? I did not want to live with the fear that should I look too closely at my Bible, I might find something I would wish I had not seen.

3. Seminary: Bible and Theology

After graduating in 1965 from Walla Walla College with a degree in theology, I went directly to the seminary at Andrews University. It was a time of turmoil there. Four teachers had come under fire for "heresy," or something similar under a more polite name. All four of them left their teaching posts; three have remained Adventists. How did they get in trouble? Here's an example: In class one day a teacher noted that the Sermon on the Mount was probably a compilation. Our hands shot up, "But Sister White says that it happened in the spring with the people seated on the grassy slopes." His comment was simple—and devastating: "I wish I could still believe like you guys do, but what can you do when you've tasted the waters of truth, and they are bitter?"

As I see it now, a both/and approach to the Sermon on the Mount—seeing it as a compilation of excerpts from a real sermon—easily resolves the dilemma. But for most deeply religious people, making peace with such an approach may take time.

Years later I had the occasion to see that man working with students in a very caring and helpful way. I got brave and reminded him of what he had said many years before. He didn't remember. But his comment was revealing: "There was a time when everything seemed to shake," he said. "But when you get your feet on the ground and know the Lord, everything changes."

In terms of my own experience with God, by far the most significant event at seminary was my "discovery" that Jesus was God incarnate, God in the flesh. But I have already told that story in chapter 6, so will move on.

4. Scotland

Our stay in Scotland for doctoral studies looms large in this story. But en route from seminary to Scotland, there were a couple of stops along the way. After completing my Bachelor of Divinity degree (now, M.Div.) in 1967, I was an intern under Arnold Kurtz at the Adventist church in

Redlands, California. It was a good experience, though tempered by the pain of the first funeral at which I officiated, a service for a six-year-old girl who died from an epileptic seizure. I barely made it through. In Scotland I would discover the honest, even violent prayers in the Bible. But those weren't mine yet, so I couldn't really pray through my grief. I have concluded that the long shadow of two Bible stories had kept my prayers polite. First, Uzzah, struck down by God for touching the ark;[5] second, the forty-two boys, mauled by two she-bears for irreverent jibes at God's prophet Elisha.[6] I wasn't about to take any risks.

The conference then sent me to Fontana, California, to pastor the Palmetto Street Church. During the two years I was there, those good people were a marvelous blessing and a help to a young, conscientious pastor. I was too energetic, too rigorous, too rigid. That's not unusual for devout people who take Ellen White seriously—but not quite seriously enough. I won't give details. But I will say that the members of the Fontana church modeled Jesus for me in a very precious way.

In 1970 I joined the School of Theology at Walla Walla College. The college expected me to finish a doctorate and promised to sponsor me for it. So after two years of teaching, we headed for the University of Edinburgh in Scotland. And that's when the fun began.

My research interests were three-fold: Old Testament, apocalyptic, and the problem of evil. Bluntly put, I was searching for a better way of explaining the tension between the violent Old Testament God and gentle Jesus. In the Old Testament, God commands His people to obliterate their enemies: "Kill their men, women, children, and even their babies."[7] And the psalmist asks God to do it for him.[8] But Jesus asks His Father to forgive His enemies[9] and commands us to love them.[10] How does one put those pieces together?

5. Living in Scotland: The Global Concern

Living in Scotland revolutionized my understanding of how to relate to the world and to the writings of Ellen White. Looking at things at the broadest level and being painfully blunt, my great challenge when we arrived in Scotland was that I just didn't feel comfortable dealing with people who weren't Adventists. I'd been a pastor, of course, and had contacts with non-Adventists all the time. But they were usually connected in some way with my work for the church. When we moved to the Walla Walla valley, we were surrounded by Adventists—some six thousand Adventists in a valley of forty thousand people. In College Place itself, where our college is located, the town may be close to 50 percent Seventh-day Adventist. By contrast, in Scotland, slightly less than three hundred Adventists live in a country of more than five million people!

During our first stay in Scotland, it was easy for me to avoid serious involvement in the larger culture. I had the perfect excuse: a Ph.D. dissertation! The whole thing troubled me, to be sure, but I didn't know how to fix it. After we returned to the States two-and-a-half years later (1974), Wanda and I talked about it and prayed about it. We found that we were both eager to go back to Scotland and give it another try, this time getting to know and love the people.

Miraculously, that's what happened, thanks in large measure to Ellen White. It was her commentary on Jesus' parable of the sheep and the goats in Matthew 25 that made the difference.[11] What liberated me were her comments about the salvation of those who have never heard the name of Christ. In "the great judgment day," she wrote, the decision turns "upon one point. . . ." The "eternal destiny" of all who stand before God "will be determined by what they have done or have neglected to do for Him in the person of the poor and suffering."[12] Then, speaking of the heathen who have never heard the name of Christ, but "who have cherished the spirit of kindness," she declares, "they will not perish."[13] 12. DA 637   13 DA 638 (1898)

But, you may ask, what does that have to do with the good Scots who couldn't begin to count the number of times they have heard the name of Christ?

Potentially, a great deal. Is God going to hold Christians accountable for right doctrine, but everyone else for right behavior? Nonsense. If I read Matthew 25 correctly, God does not ask doctrinal questions of anyone. The same standard, the same question, applies to everyone, whether or not they have heard the name of Jesus or followed Him knowingly.

Much to my chagrin, what I discovered in working through this "problem" was a lingering suspicion, buried deep in my soul (I would never have said it out loud), that I had to convince others to keep the Sabbath and become Seventh-day Adventists if they were to be saved. The really troubling part of that perspective is suggested by Ezekiel 3: If they are lost because I didn't warn them, I will be lost, too.

At the same time, however, if I turned the tables and asked how I would want other people to treat me, I knew I would have been repulsed if others approached me with the conviction that they were irrevocably right and that I had to see it their way in order to be saved. By pointing me to Scripture, Ellen White helped me put the matter to rest. Scripture, of course, is abundantly clear. I just couldn't see it.

But once I had seen the light, I knew we could return to Scotland and with eagerness. This time we would get to know and love the people— while hoping like everything that they could discover and accept what was so precious to us. The difference was that now I could love them, entice them toward the "truth," without feeling that I had to be coercive. My own doctrinal convictions remained solid. I had not compromised an iota on that score. The only difference—and it was huge—was that, before, I felt (at a very deep, virtually subconscious level) that I had to force them, push them, or even frighten them. No wonder I buried myself in my dissertation. Now I could leave all that forceful stuff in the hands of the Spirit. That's His business, not mine. I would witness; the Spirit would convict.

A reflection: I suspect many Adventists are quite ready to see the good heathen in the kingdom—we're just not so sure about the good Baptist or the good Catholic. I think I discovered vestiges of that kind of thinking in my soul before the Lord used Matthew 25 and *The Desire of Ages* to root it out.

We did go back to Scotland in 1979 and developed some enduring friendships with a Church of Scotland pastor and his wife, a Christian Science couple, a Plymouth Brethren family, indeed their extended family. We had a great time. I believe we were able to come much closer to Jesus' ideal, i.e., treating others as we would have wanted them to treat us if we were in their place. In short, as far as I was concerned, Jesus' second great command had finally come home to my heart: "You shall love your neighbor as yourself."[14]

6. Living in Scotland: Adventist Lifestyle Stuff

Turning now from that more global concern, let me open a window for you on the life and thinking of a devout, conscientious, conservative Adventist who moves to Scotland from an Adventist ghetto in the States.

Remember, this was early 1970s; some of these issues would certainly be less acute some thirty years later. But at that time, we tussled with four major hurdles—and the words "tussle" and "hurdle" are not at all too strong. I list the issues here in order, based on the intensity with which I experienced them, from least intense to most intense. Wanda's order would be different. Those familiar with the writings of Ellen White will know that all four concerns are rooted in a "conservative" approach to her writings.

Church school. In a sense, this was the easiest issue we dealt with in Scotland, for there were—and are—no Adventist church schools in that country. On our first visit there, we managed to avoid the problem because our girls were young (four and six) when we returned home. The Scots, however, start their children in school at age four-and-a-half, barely able to toddle, it seemed to us. We had no burden to push our girls into an accelerated school program so decided simply to let school wait until we returned to the States. Ironically, it was the Adventist pastor who noted our civil disobedience: "It's the law, you know," he reminded us. We knew, but chose to remain disobedient.

On later visits (1979 and 1984), school did become an issue since our girls were older, and we were there for six months. We briefly contemplated the equivalent of "public school," but elected to send our girls to a private school for girls instead. One brief visit to the public school convinced us that it would be far too raw for our gentle two.

So on the issue of church schools, we rather quickly adapted to the "practical" rather than holding out for the "ideal." The "ideal" option simply wasn't there.

Country living. When we first arrived in Scotland, we ended up renting a semidetached bungalow (= duplex) in a nice neighborhood on the south side of Edinburgh. But it was a difficult adjustment for Wanda, who had grown up in semirural Oregon. When we got serious about exploring rural options, the realities of life in Britain began to sink home. At that time, we learned, the standard housing density for new construction was seventeen dwelling units per acre. Development land cost the equivalent of US$50,000 per acre; the average weekly income was the equivalent of one hundred dollars. In short, if you wanted to live in the country, you had to be wealthy enough to buy a whole estate.

In our case, we were temporary residents and had more options. So we went on the search for a place in the country, running an ad in *The Scotsman* newspaper: "Wanted: Country cottage for long let." We saw some amazing places, but ended up with one that was nearly ideal, a former gardener's cottage on a small estate south of Edinburgh. We even had our own private woods. It was wonderful. But by this time we realized that this "ideal" would be virtually impossible for the typical Scottish family.

That wasn't as clear to others, however. I well remember the Sabbath afternoon discussions with another Adventist couple, a British multi-generational Adventist pastor, married to a first-generation American Adventist. They were actually living in the city—the "practical"—while arguing that they really should be living in the country—the "ideal"—as per Ellen White's counsel. We were living in the country—the "ideal"—while arguing that this "ideal" would be impossible for most Scots; they would have to live in the city—the "practical."

So on the issue of country living, we were able to find a way to live the "ideal," but had made the mental adjustment which allowed us to defend and support the "practical."

Wedding ring. Now we're into rough waters. Initially, neither Wanda nor I felt any need to wear a wedding ring. None of our parents had ever worn one. Furthermore, in America in the early 1970s, everyone "knew" that only "liberated" Adventists wore the wedding ring. It was a symbol of their rebellion against the church. We weren't rebels (though in a sense, I am a rebel, just a very obedient one).

But Wanda was observant. One day she commented to the wife of the Adventist pastor, "I notice that most married women wear the wedding ring." Immediate correction: "Not most, all!"

Not encouraging. Time for a second opinion, this time from an Adventist university student. He was bright, British, generally positive towards things American, and a committed Adventist Christian. His response came without hesitation: "If Wanda doesn't wear a wedding ring, your children will be considered illegitimate." Not good news.

Being rather thrifty folk (unofficially Scottish in that respect), we decided to try the cheap route, an inexpensive ring from Woolworths. Bad fit.

The only option left was a real jeweler's shop and a proper wedding ring.

We tried to look dignified and self-confident, but it was tough, especially with our two little girls tagging along. Given our impulses toward thrift and modesty, it felt like I was saying: "Give us the smallest, cheapest, ring you have." Really crass! Of course, we didn't say it quite that way, but that's what it felt like. The experience was awkward and painful. The scene in the jeweler's shop in Edinburgh is still a vivid one in my mind's eye.

But it worked. We got the ring. Wanda began wearing it immediately, and it quickly became just part of our daily scenery. When our American Adventist friends would visit us, however, they were sure that we had abandoned the faith.

There is also a fascinating German postscript to this story. In the 1970s in Britain, for some reason, only the married Adventist women wore the ring; married Adventist men typically did not. But when we hatched the idea of spending a year in Germany, I somehow learned that in Germany both husband and wife wear the wedding ring—and with conviction. So when everything was in order for us to spend the 1980-81 school year at Marienhöhe Seminary in Darmstadt, Germany, where I would be an exchange teacher, I decided that I, too, would buy a wedding ring and wear it.

I completely forgot—until we were in the Seattle-Tacoma airport, en route to Germany. A quick search of airport shops turned up a six-dollar ring with a one-year guarantee. I grabbed it (after all, I would only need it for a year). It was too broad and shiny for the prevailing standards of modesty at our house, but I wore it anyway, and the shine from a six-dollar ring quickly mellows out!

We didn't explore the wedding ring rationale while we were in Germany. But after we returned, I gained some insight from a conversation that grew out of a seminar I was holding at the Valley View Adventist Church in Medford, Oregon (1984). The seminar itself was going well. Southern Oregon is solid conservative country. But I enjoy working with conservatives, not only because I know them to be kindred spirits, but because they are so responsive. An academic crowd just sits there with arms folded, and you seldom know what they're *really* thinking. Believers show it all over; you *always* know when you have pushed them too far. When the nodding stops, when faces and knuckles turn white, you know it's time to back up and tell another story.

In this instance I can still clearly picture the audience, especially the man in the third pew on the right side. He seemed to me to be of head-elder caliber: thoughtful, sober, dignified. I had my eye on him as I told my wedding ring story. When I got to the line about the illegitimate children, he began to nod slowly. Success.

After that meeting a German woman (married to an American) came up to me and asked if I knew why Adventists in Germany felt so strongly about wearing the wedding ring. I told her I didn't know. "It has to do with *Fasching*," she said, "the festival month preceding Lent. During *Fasching*, married people take off their wedding rings and play around. When Lent comes, they put them back on and do penance."

No wonder devout German Christians who cherish the marriage relationship insist on wearing the wedding ring thirteen months in the year!

Eating between meals. If the wedding ring was heavy weather for me, eating between meals was the eye of the storm. Ellen White's statement seems so categorical, so absolute: "Never let a morsel pass your lips between your regular meals."[15]

The trouble is that in Scotland, a visit to anyone's home at any hour of the day or night is a call for food. It may be just a snack, but it is always at least a morsel! We could politely refuse, of course (and sometimes did), but it felt very awkward to do so.

For us, the crucible that brought the issue from simmer to boil was the Friday night youth fellowship in Edinburgh. With so few Adventists in Scotland, the Sabbath hours together were especially precious. The church families agreed to open their homes to the young people on Friday evenings during the dark winter months. We developed a rotation, car pooling it to a different home each week and starting over again after we had made the rounds. Right at the beginning, we agreed that we would finish about 9:00 P.M. with something to drink. After all, we already would have had our supper. "Fine," said our Scottish hostesses. "Something to drink." (Note: In very conservative Adventist circles, juice is also off-limits between meals, for juice is simply a liquified morsel. A morsel is a morsel is a morsel. Always.)

I well remember that first fellowship at the Gulland home. Sister Ann Gulland owned and operated a thriving health food shop adjacent to the

Adventist church in downtown Edinburgh. When we finished our discussion at 9:00 P.M., she invited us into the dining room for "a little something to drink." Indeed. Here was "something to drink," all right—and fruit, nuts, soups, sandwiches, cookies, cakes. It was a stunning spread. You can easily imagine the tears streaming down the faces of the university students who had survived on their own cooking during the week.

Everyone had a good time, as I recall. We didn't make any comments, didn't raise any waves at that point. The others ate. We had something to drink.

But that night when we went home, I opened my Bible to Romans 14 and began a titanic struggle with myself, my Bible, and my God. Ellen White was part of the picture, too, of course, for she was the cause of the "problem." Less intense people will listen with amazement to all this. But hear me out. I will help you understand what I write and why.

These are the key phrases confronting me from Romans 14, cited here from the Revised Standard Version, the Bible I was using at the time: "Let us no more pass judgment on one another, but rather decide never to put a stumbling block or hindrance in the way of a brother. . . . If your brother is being injured by what you eat [read: 'what you don't eat'] you are no longer walking in love. Do not let what you eat [read: 'don't eat'] cause the ruin of one for whom Christ died. . . . For the kingdom of God does not mean food and drink but righteousness and peace and joy in the Holy Spirit. . . . Do not for the sake of food destroy the work of God."[16]

Now in Romans 14, Paul isn't talking at all about eating between meals, but about the ceremonial distinction between clean and unclean foods. Health is not an issue; Paul never uses health-related arguments, such as "live longer and more happily." In Romans he is talking about the tensions created between Jews over clean and unclean foods. In Corinthians 8 and 10, he uses the same principles to address the Jewish-Gentile tension over food offered to idols. Yet the underlying principle in both contexts is that people are more important than food! And that's why I couldn't escape Romans 14 when dealing with the issue of eating between meals.

I raised the issue quietly with Alan Hodges, now British Union ministerial secretary, but then the young associate pastor who was helping with the youth. I wasn't bombastic, but I was earnest. The youth fellowships continued.

Others ate; I had something to drink. Over the next few weeks, however, our conversation gradually seeped out to touch others in the group and the influence began to be felt. The results were not very pretty. Our hostesses still fed us bounteously, but everyone was eating less, just enough to be polite, it seemed to me. And joy had taken a real hit. Food and drink are so important to fellowship. And our fellowship wasn't nearly as much fun as it had been at the beginning.

I could see all that, but didn't know what to do about it—not yet. I was haunted almost constantly by the lines from Romans 14. The Adventists in the Edinburgh church were gracious to us. Nobody reprimanded us for rigidity. We rarely talked about "the problem," certainly not in depth. But I kept tussling with myself, my Bible, and my God—and, of course, with Ellen White.

The turning point came one Friday night at the home of Sister Lean, a new Adventist who ran a small guest house in Edinburgh. Out of love, she had prepared a heaping tray of sandwiches for us. But that evening appetites were restrained: a wee nibble here, a small bite there. I vividly remember the puzzled look on her face and the touch of hurt in her voice as she commented, "Nobody must be very hungry tonight." It was like a dagger to my soul. This precious child of God had opened up her home, her kitchen, and her heart to us, and we were turning away. I sensed that we could cause eternal damage to this soul for whom Christ died.

The time had come. I'd done my homework, in my Bible, on my knees; I knew Romans 14 through and through by now. And I knew what I had to do. So I led the charge, and we polished off the sandwiches—all of them. It was the right thing to do. I knew it then without a doubt, and I know it still.

To sum it up, people are infinitely more important than my own "ideal" habits. Jesus knew that and taught it; Paul knew that and taught it; and Ellen White would come to understand it and teach it. Jesus and Paul have been a great blessing to me. So has Ellen White. And being able to trace *how* Ellen White came to grasp what Jesus and Paul taught, has helped me, a rock-ribbed conservative, to see it, too. And not only to see it, but to believe it.

Conclusion

What we had been learning in Scotland was how to apply Ellen White's counsel in time and place. Even seemingly absolute statements had to be seen in terms of context and need. Later a student would exclaim in class, "What you are talking about is the difference between a casebook and a codebook." Immediately I saw the light, and I've used that idea ever since. But I have been amazed at how much turmoil that distinction has caused in some Adventist circles. I address the casebook/codebook distinction further in chapter 9.

If we can grasp Ellen White's view of law, however, it provides the perfect tool for helping us to know how to apply her counsel in a helpful way, and also an important tool for understanding some of the remarkable changes that she makes in her writings over the course of her life.

The next two chapters address those issues. The first one, chapter 9, explores the question of "law"; the second, chapter 10, focuses specifically on the changing perspectives and interpretation in Ellen White's writings, showing how her understanding of law makes good sense out of what she actually does in her writings.

---

[1] *Testimonies for the Church*, vol. 3, p. 373 (1870).

[2] *Testimonies for the Church*, vol. 9, p. 162 (1909): "The time will come when we may have to discard some of the articles of diet we now use, such as milk and cream and eggs; but it is not necessary to bring upon ourselves perplexity by premature and extreme restrictions. Wait until the circumstances demand it and the Lord prepares the way for it."

[3] "Carlyle, Thomas," in E. A. Livingstone, ed., *The Oxford Dictionary of the Christian Church*, third ed., (New York: Oxford University Press, 1997), p. 288.

[4] *Messages to Young People* was compiled by the "Young People's Society of Missionary Volunteers," not by the White Estate, and was published in 1930.

[5] 2 Samuel 6.

[6] 2 Kings 2.

[7] 1 Samuel 15:3, CEV.

[8] Cf. Psalm 69:22–28.

[9] Luke 23:34.

[10] Matthew 5:44; Luke 6:27.

[11] *The Desire of Ages*, pp. 637–641 (1898).

[12] *Ibid.*, p. 637 (1898).

[13] *Ibid.*, p. 638 (1898).

[14] Matthew 22:39.

[15] *Testimonies for the Church*, vol. 3, p. 373 (1870).

[16] Romans 14:13–20, excerpts, RSV.

CHAPTER 9

From Codebook to Casebook to Jesus

"Shouldn't we do what the Bible says?" he asked.

"What do you mean?" I queried.

"Well, the Bible says that a woman should not teach or exercise authority over a man."[1]

"You're right, it does say that," I responded. "But can you think of any place in the Bible where a woman does teach or exercise authority over a man?"

"Well, yes."

"Then shouldn't we treat the passage about women not teaching or having authority as having local rather than universal application?"

"All right," he agreed. And we moved to another topic.

A few moments later, virtually the same question came up in connection with another topic and another passage in Scripture. "Shouldn't we do what the Bible says?"

"Can you think of any examples in the Bible . . . ?"

"Well, yes."

"Then shouldn't we treat that passage as having local rather than universal application?" I asked again.

And so the conversation went. Again and again we went through that cycle. It was remarkable.

A weekend visitor to our valley, this young pastor and his wife were staying at the home of a mutual friend who had invited me over to meet him. Bright, devout, and thoroughly familiar with his Bible, this young man had been a convert to Adventism some years earlier and was en route to a new pastorate at a church that was divided over the question of local women elders. He was grappling with the practical implications of that issue.

I had slipped over on a Sabbath afternoon, intending to stay no more than a half hour or forty-five minutes. I ended up staying four hours. In addition to the constant recycling of the question, "Shouldn't we do what the Bible says?" two other parts of that long conversation stand out for me, both of them illustrating how difficult—even painful—it is to bring reason to bear on what we believe to be commands from the Lord.

After we had cycled and recycled his question many times, I noticed something intriguing about his Bible: numerous carefully drawn red circles around certain verse numbers. So I asked him what that meant.

Somewhat sheepishly he told me: "Every time I find a verse that doesn't fit my system, I draw a red circle around the verse number."

So, in effect, what we had been doing all afternoon was going from red circle to red circle. I never once caught him by surprise by any of the passages I called to his attention. He had always been there before and had added the red circle.

He was deeply committed to being faithful in his walk with God, but didn't know what to do about all the bits and pieces in his Bible that didn't fit his system. He hadn't tossed them yet, but he knew they were there. He was troubled, but not yet ready to buy into a clear-cut "casebook" approach to divine commands and prophetic counsel.

Later in this chapter, we will look more closely at the casebook approach. In this instance it was actually the casebook idea that led to the other memorable aspect of our conversation. In my view, it was becoming more and more evident that everyone lives out a casebook approach in life, but some find it very difficult to admit it. Put another way, everyone practices what I preach; they just don't want to hear it preached! Given my own experiences with resistance to the idea, I decided to try a modest little experiment. For some time I had been mulling over possible illustrations that could help us understand the nature of the resistance to a casebook approach to the Bible. Why does it feel so dangerous, at least to some?

Convinced that he was a devout and conscientious Christian, deeply earnest about being faithful to his Lord, I decided to try this one out on him: "To adopt a casebook approach to the Bible," I said, "feels like you are standing nose-to-nose with your dad, saying: I know you said to do this, Dad, but I'm not going to do it because it doesn't apply to me."

"That's exactly right!" he exclaimed passionately. "That's just what it feels like."

Before he left town the next morning, I called him up to make a suggestion: "When you come to a conclusion about such things as we discussed yesterday," I said, "particularly when the biblical evidence is clear that a particular passage must be local rather than universal in application, write it down so that you can remember what you have decided."

"Well, I'm going to have to do something," he said with a hint of a chuckle. "There are just too many verses that don't fit into my system."

We prayed, and I wished him well in his new pastorate. We've only had occasional contact since then. I understand that his church is doing well under his leadership. I don't know what he has done about all his little red circles.

Commands in the Bible, Counsel From Ellen White

My young pastor friend was grappling with issues raised by the Bible. As noted in the last chapter, the challenges we faced in Scotland were ones raised by Ellen White's counsel. The common ground was and is that in both of our situations we felt a deep-seated need to be faithful to God by "obeying" specific commands and specific counsels, even when it became clear that they didn't "work." Were we being rebellious, disobedient, or wicked by not following the letter of the law in each case, even though our reason told us that an exception would be quite appropriate?

What I know best is my own reaction. And I can testify that it took much struggling and prayer on my part before I was ready to eat between meals and do so conscientiously. What did God think about my action? Can Scripture and/or the writings of Ellen White help us in this dilemma? The defining moment for me came when I saw that Sister Lean, the hostess who was graciously ministering to our needs, could be put at risk by my personal convictions. To this day, I am convinced that I did the right thing by eating between meals in those circumstances.

The justification for my change of heart came directly from a biblical book and chapter: Romans 14. In one of the other Scottish situations we faced, the matter of how to relate to our non-Adventist friends in Scotland, the solution was mediated by Ellen White through chapter 70 in *The Desire of Ages,* her commentary on the great judgment scene in Matthew 25. The words of Ellen White were a great help, but she actually pointed to a key biblical passage as the basis for her comments. I continue to be impressed with how often the Bible and the writings of Ellen White can interact in positive ways, with either one or both providing the clue that points toward the solution.

The Key Issue: Authority

The underlying issue, it seems to me, is the question of "authority." Whether one is confronting Scripture or the writings of Ellen White, the same principles will be at work to determine our conclusion. Living in Scotland forced us to face the hard questions of how to apply the counsels of Ellen White in real life situations. Yet the adjustments we made as a result of our stay in Scotland would have been seen by many devout Adventists as serious compromises of the faith. That would have been more true in the early 1970s than it would be now.

Ironically, I have decided that the best description of that "obedient" attitude comes from the Bible, but not from those who worship the true God in heaven. I am thinking of the "secular" attitude toward royal laws reflected in the books of Daniel and Esther. In Daniel 6, Daniel ends up in the lions' den because the laws of the Medes and the Persians "cannot be changed"; and in Esther 8, Esther's people are put at risk because an edict sealed with the king's ring "cannot be revoked." That was true even though both kings involved, Darius and Ahasuerus, discovered that the laws had been devised with evil intent. And in each case, the king who made the law was powerless to change it.[2]

That attitude of absolute obedience toward authority is also reflected in the way the early Old Testament narratives deal with oaths and the spoken word. In Genesis 27, Jacob deceives his father Isaac into giving him the birthright blessing. But even when Isaac discovers the deception, the spoken blessing cannot be changed.[3]

That same unbending attitude toward the authority of the spoken word figures prominently in two incidents which rank first and second in my list of "worst" Old Testament stories. The "second-worst" story begins in Joshua 9 and tells how the Gibeonites tricked Joshua and the Israelites into making a

---

treaty with them. The treaty with the Gibeonites was locked in place because Israel had "sworn to them by the LORD, the God of Israel."[4] The sequel of this "second-worst" story comes in 2 Samuel 21 which describes how King Saul later broke that treaty and the LORD sent a famine on the land to remind the Israelites of their promise. King David had to put things right before God would heal the land. The Gibeonites set the terms: Hand over seven sons of Saul "and we will impale them before the LORD at Gibeon."[5]

The first-place winner in my "worst" story competition, the narrative of the dismembered concubine in Judges 19–21, also illustrates the idea of the immoveable oath. When all the blood and mayhem was over, Israel still needed two hundred women to add to the four hundred virgins they had captured from Jabesh-Gilead to provide wives for the Benjaminites. Because Israel had sworn not to give wives to Benjamin from their own people, they advised the remaining Benjaminite bachelors to go to Shiloh at the time of the annual festival of the LORD, hide in the vineyards, then snatch a dancing maiden for a wife. If the fathers or brothers complained, Israel promised to use this logic: "Be generous and allow us to have them; because we did not capture in battle a wife for each man. But neither did you incur guilt by giving your daughters to them."[6] In each of these biblical examples, the law or the oath remained firmly in place, even though it had been formulated as a result of deception or ill-advised passion (as in the case of the Benjaminite wives).

The point of all this is that the struggles which we went through in Scotland over Ellen White's counsels, and the struggles confronting our young pastor friend, are not unique, but are deeply rooted in our sinful human condition. In Adventism, that earnest desire to be faithful to authority triggers an oft-repeated pattern among those who are most serious about following all of Ellen White's counsels—a move away from the rest of the world. These devout, conscientious people tend to gravitate toward small Adventist enclaves out in the country so that they can concentrate on obeying the Lord without being distracted by modern culture and other people.

The Way Out: From Sacred Authority to Sanctified Reason

Based on reactions to other things I have written, I know that a primary objection to my approach to law, indeed to the way I approach Scripture as a whole, is formulated in terms of exalting reason over revelation.

Do Scripture and the writings of Ellen White address that issue? Yes, in a variety of ways, and we'll look at those. But first let me suggest two conclusions that have come clear in my mind about the overall thrust of the biblical message. They both have to do with authority:

1. Sin tragically distorts our view of authority; this is, perhaps, one of its most significant and deadly results.

2. Jesus came to reclaim a proper understanding of authority; this is one of the most significant purposes of the Incarnation.

In what follows I briefly outline my reasons for these conclusions, pointing to specific passages of Scripture for support and illustration.

Old Testament: Authority Figures Become Violent and Arbitrary

The examples cited earlier in this chapter illustrate how "obedience" to authority had taken on a fixed and unbending character in the Old Testament, even if it was obedience to the impersonal authority of the spoken word (blessings, oaths). Three features mark the development of Old Testament attitudes:

1. **Fear, the starting point.** When our first parents sinned in the Garden of Eden, the picture of God presented in Genesis 3 is a very gentle one. He simply goes for His regular walk and misses His friends. "Where are you, Adam?" He calls. Adam answers, admitting that he hid because he was afraid.[7] The other catastrophic results of sin flow out of that fearful beginning.

2. **Violent reactions, violent punishments, violent authorities.** If fear was the first recorded result of sin in Genesis 3, bloodshed followed hard on its heels as God provided skins for Adam and Eve and Abel brought an animal sacrifice. But bloodshed soon goes beyond animals. Cain murders his brother and revels in an over-the-top vengeance: "I have killed a man for wounding me."[8] By the time of the Exodus, Mosaic law seeks to limit bloodshed by invoking the eye-for-an-eye law of revenge.[9] But the same Mosaic code mandates the death penalty for breaking every one of the Ten Commandments except the last one (coveting). And when Israel embarked on

an unauthorized celebration at the foot of Mt. Sinai, Moses' reaction was quick. Strap on your swords, he told the faithful Levites, "kill your brother, your friend, and your neighbor."[10] When Joshua took over from Moses, the people declared their allegiance in absolute terms: "Whoever rebels against your orders and disobeys your words, whatever you command, shall be put to death."[11] In Joshua 7 Israel stones Achan and his family; in 1 Samuel 15, Samuel hews Agag in pieces before the Lord; and in 1 Kings 18 Elijah kills four hundred fifty prophets of Baal. Religious liberty obviously didn't rank high in Israel's lists of values.

3. **Violent worship.** In the biblical account of human history, both the expectation and the reality of violence become increasingly clear. And not only are human authorities expected to be violent, the God/gods standing behind them are too. With the passage of time, human imagination seemingly generated ever stronger expectations of violence in both human and divine authorities. Adam's fear was producing its deadly fruit.

Thus, in order to reach people who expected divine beings to be violent, the great God of heaven used language and actions that they could understand. Early on, animal sacrifices became part of the worship scene; even child sacrifice lurked nearby. God took steps to restrain this most violent of all acts of worship, commanding Abraham to sacrifice Isaac, but then providing a substitute at the last minute,[12] a tantalizing foreshadowing of the One who would bring all sacrifices of all kinds to an end by His own sacrificial death.

Still, when Israel left Egypt, God commanded that an animal be substituted for every firstborn,[13] showing that the threat of child sacrifice was a real one. In Judges 11, Jephthah the judge sacrificed his daughter because of his oath; in 2 Kings 3, the king of Moab frightened away the Israelite invaders by offering up his firstborn son, the crown prince;[14] Manasseh, whose fifty-five-year reign was the longest of any king of Judah, also offered up his son,[15] even the prophet Micah put child sacrifice at the top of his list of potential sacrifices: "Shall I give my firstborn for my transgression, the fruit of my body for the sin of my soul?"[16]

To sum up, the Old Testament is thoroughly authoritarian and heavily imprinted with fear and violence. One doesn't need to think; one obeys, no

Is that the way God planned it?

questions asked. That helps explain why, at Sinai, *the revelation of God in the Old Testament*, God revealed Himself in such a violent way, ordering, for example, the death of any creature, animal or human, that got too close to the mountain.

Early Hints of a Casebook Approach?

As authoritarian as the Old Testament appears to have been, still, in certain notable cases, consideration for human feelings and passions did force a way around the "unchanging" law. The result was a kind of primitive "casebook" approach. That's what happened when the Israelites offered the Benjaminites an alternative way of acquiring wives so that no one would be guilty of breaking the oath.[17] An even more visceral illustration of passion over oath is provided by the people of Israel when Saul uttered a rash oath, invoking the death penalty on anyone who ate anything before sundown that day. When Jonathan, in ignorance, broke the oath, eating some honey, Saul vowed to put his son to death. The people stood in his way: "As the LORD lives, not one hair of his head shall fall to the ground; for he has worked with God today. So the people ransomed Jonathan and he did not die."[18]

In addition to these notable exceptions to oaths, however, there is abundant evidence that even in the Old Testament, a casebook approach prevailed in everyday life. That becomes clearest in the book of Proverbs where seemingly contradictory sayings appear back to back: "Do not answer fools according to their folly. . . ." and "Answer fools according to their folly. . . ."[19] But legal codes are much more subtle. Apparently, in an authoritarian system, formally defining a casebook approach *seems* to undermine obedience to law.

The New Testament is another matter, however, for Jesus' vision points to a radical transformation of ideas about authority and obedience. Understanding that transformation is crucial if we want a truly Christian approach to obedience today. It is also crucial for understanding Ellen White's writings and experience, especially in light of the transformation of her own understanding of Jesus, seeing Him no longer simply as the subordinate Son of God, but as God incarnate, the possessor of "life, original, unborrowed, underived."[20]

New Testament: Authority Transformed

But if we are in the business of contrasting the Testaments, it is helpful to note that the authority of Jesus is on our side, for Jesus Himself explicitly endorsed such contrasts, indeed formulated the contrasts Himself. At the same time, however, He placed the contrasts within the context of the enduring authority of the Old Testament, the only Bible that Jesus and the apostles had.

All this comes clear in the Sermon on the Mount in Matthew 5. Six times Jesus declares, "You have heard. . . , but I say." All of the contrasts include elements from the Old Testament, and, in some cases, additional traditional sayings, followed by Jesus' "fresh" interpretation that emphasizes the "spirit" of the law, rather than the often misleading "letter." But all of these contrasts fall under the all-important heading provided by Matthew 5:17: "Do not think that I have come to abolish the law or the prophets; I have come not to abolish but to fulfill." In a very real sense, Jesus is "filling" the Old Testament law "full" of new and deeper meaning. Thus He shows how it is possible to contrast the old and the new, filling it full of something new and fresh, but without in any way abolishing the old.

So with that "permission" from Jesus firmly in hand, let's note the striking differences between His message and mission and the dominant thrust of the Old Testament.

1. **Love in place of fear.** The most vivid formulation of this contrast is found in 1 John 4:18, "Perfect love casts out fear." Instead of confronting the weak and the evil with raw power and force, Jesus sought to win through the patient practice of gentle love. He could still be forceful in rebuking evil, especially when it threatened the weak and vulnerable. And He could warn of fearful consequences. But in His personal presence He modeled the power of goodness rather than raw, fearful power. Perhaps most memorable here is the way He urged us to love our enemies and the way He practiced what He preached throughout His ministry, even when hanging on the cross.

2. **Forgiveness, not just punishment; serving instead of being served.** "Turn the other cheek." "Go the second mile." "Stand up, take your mat, and walk." "Neither do I condemn you. Go your way, and from now on do

not sin again." The forgiveness which Jesus brought and taught was certainly not anything new. But what made it so fresh and attractive was to see it offered with such gentleness and grace, to find it packaged with such hope by One whose presence did not overpower with fear, but awed with the radiance of pure goodness.

When He walked on earth as God in the flesh, Jesus never killed anyone, never even struck anyone; when His anger burned against greed and hypocrisy displayed in the temple courtyard, the power of that beautiful anger was irresistible to the children, the blind, and the lame, and they came running to Him.[21] I wish I knew how to be angry like that.

But perhaps Jesus' most powerful and transforming words were the ones He spoke to all His disciples after two of them, James and John, had come with their mother, and in good Old Testament fashion, asked for the top places in the kingdom. Jesus' words deserve boldface type:

> You know that the rulers of the Gentiles lord it over them, and their high officials exercise authority over them. Not so with you. Instead, whoever wants to become great among you must be your servant, and whoever wants to be first must be your slave—just as the Son of Man did not come to be served, but to serve, and to give his life as a ransom for many.—Matthew 20:25–28, NIV.

The greatest power in those words is packed into the last sentence. For, if we ask, Who was and is the Son of Man? We must answer, "Jesus." And who was Jesus? God in human flesh. Thus, when God comes to show us what He is really like, He does not come demanding worship or service. He simply comes to serve. And the full fruit of His mission becomes clear only when we see Him live out His message so fully that He is willing to die on Golgotha's cross for us.

Put very bluntly, at Sinai, God came to kill. At Golgotha, God came to die. But not just to die, to live again so that we, too, could walk in the footsteps of the Master, living in love and living in hope that someday He would return as He promised, restoring the world to innocence and beauty so that we might live with Him and with all His children throughout all eternity.

He did all that to show us that people are the most important part of God's creation, that people are more important than rules—but also to show us that rules help us to know how to treat people. And so the New Testament teaches us a casebook approach, but one that is fully anchored in God's loving character and in the unchanging principles of His law.

In an authoritarian system, a personal hierarchy of values develops with great difficulty because one is so thoroughly aware of a hierarchy of people and authorities. And when the system is fully in place, one doesn't have to think, just obey. Jesus came to teach us that loving is the highest form of obedience. And how do we love? By thinking about all that God has done through the millennia and praying that His Spirit will guide us in applying this knowledge to the people with whom we come in contact. In a perfect world, such applications will come naturally, even without thinking. That's a promise that even the Old Testament people knew about: "No longer shall they teach one another, or say to each other, Know the LORD," wrote Jeremiah, "for they shall all know me, from the least of them to the greatest, says the Lord."[22]

Casebook in the New Testament: Worshiping God by Serving People

When listing above the primary features of the Old Testament understanding of "authority," my third characteristic was "violent worship." I have decided to break ranks with my tidy organization and give the New Testament counterpart greater visibility with its own heading. The transformation in the understanding of authority in the New Testament is especially significant when it comes to worship. I want that to be very clear, even in the form of the printed text.

In our modern world, "conservatives" typically focus on their responsibility to God—the most extreme example of that impulse is the horrific 9/11 "act of worship," performed in the name of God and resulting in the deaths of some three thousand innocent people. God is everything; people are nothing.

By contrast, liberals often slight the vertical dimension and simply focus on the horizontal. In extreme cases, the vertical dimension is fully denied. The cover blurb on Lloyd Graham's book, *Deceptions and Myths,* cited in chapter 4, illustrates that position: "Mr. Graham believes it is time this scriptural tyranny was broken so that we may devote our time to man instead of God and to civilizing ourselves instead of saving our souls that were never lost."[23]

What I find so intriguing and helpful about Ellen White's mature perspective (that is, after she had experienced the power of knowing that Jesus was God incarnate) is the fact that she discovered in the New Testament that the best way to serve God is to serve humanity.[24]

That idea, to be sure, is already forcefully presented in the Old Testament. One thinks immediately of Isaiah 58: "Is not this the fast that I choose: to loose the bonds of injustice, to undo the thongs of the yoke, to let the oppressed go free, and to break every yoke?"[25] But what is so powerful about that message when it comes through Jesus, is that we see God Himself modeling this service to humanity. There is still a place for ritual, for singing, for praying, for acts and words of praise poured out directly to God. But all this should result in service to those in need. In the Old Testament, the prophets' strongest words against ritual were spoken when the people practiced the ritual while oppressing their fellow human beings.[26]

In arguing that the New Testament more clearly illustrates the principle that people are more important than rules, several key contexts stand out. I will note these briefly below in the order in which they appear in the New Testament, with a brief comment accompanying each:

Matthew 7:12. "In everything do to others as you would have them do to you; for this is the law and the prophets." Here is the briefest of all summaries of the Old Testament: Treat people right, that is, the way you would have them treat you if you were in their place. As lived out in the Old Testament itself, that could mean a touch of violence if that was what the people were expecting from their authority figures.

Matthew 22:37–40. "You shall love the Lord your God with all your heart, and with all your soul, and with all your mind. This is the greatest and first commandment. And a second is like it: You shall love your neighbor as yourself. On these two commandments hang all the law and the prophets." Although Jesus is quoting Old Testament passages, what is different is the clear introduction of a three-level hierarchy of values: Greatest, next greatest, and everything else, "hanging" or dependent upon these two.

The authoritarian structure of the Old Testament, built around a hierarchy of leaders, made it almost impossible to develop the concept of a hierarchy of values that would call for decisions by the individual. But in Jesus' kingdom, where even the leader is a servant, a hierarchy of values becomes essential and points toward a casebook approach.

Mark 2:27, 28. "The sabbath was made for humankind, and not humankind for the sabbath; so the Son of Man is lord even of the sabbath." The main thrust of this passage is also reflected in the parallels found in Matthew 12 and Luke 6. The disciples have plucked grain on the Sabbath, thereby triggering the wrath of the authorities. Jesus not only defends the disciples, He proceeds with one of His Sabbath miracles, healing a man's withered hand, a miracle that could have been performed just as easily on any other day. Indeed, all five of Jesus' Sabbath healing miracles could be cited here.[27]

What is so remarkable about Jesus' response to His objectors when the disciples picked some grain on Sabbath is the Old Testament example He cites in His and their defense, namely, the story of David eating consecrated bread from the sanctuary. According to Jesus' words in the Gospels, that was an unlawful act, but still justified because human need takes precedence over law. As the story is told originally in 1 Samuel 21, David gained access to the bread through deceit, and the end result was the massacre of the priests at Nob. Only Abiathar escaped with his life. Given the deceit at the beginning and the massacre at the end, Jesus' use of the story is indeed remarkable.

Acts 10; 11; 14; 15. In Acts 10 and 11, four key events follow one right after the other: (1) God's appearance to the Gentile Cornelius, promising him help; (2) Peter's three-fold vision of the unclean creatures, teaching him that the Gentiles are equals in Christ; (3) Peter's visit to the group of Gentile believers meeting with Cornelius; (4) Peter's defense of his actions before the Christian leaders in Jerusalem. These events take place perhaps some eight to ten years after the Resurrection.

Then, perhaps some six to eight years after that cluster of events, Acts 14 and 15 reports how Paul's successful evangelistic mission to the Gentiles triggered strong reaction among Jews who believed the Gentiles must first be circumcised before they could become Christians. The story of the Jerusalem conference follows, where, under the guidance of the Spirit, the believers agree that Gentiles can be accepted, without circumcision, as equals in Christ.

What is notable about this sequence of events is the way it illustrates the slow and painful struggle in the early church over the question of Gentile equality in the church. Instead of changes in "law" being immediate and self-evident following Jesus' death and resurrection, they were still being hotly debated nearly twenty years later. When the matter was finally settled, it came about not by vision or mandate—though a vision had nudged Peter in the right direction—but by discussion and mutual agreement. Equality had been reached: "We believe that we will be saved through the grace of Lord Jesus, just as they will."[28] And it happened on the basis of Spirit-led discussion: "For it has seemed good to the Holy Spirit and to us. . . ."[29] Ellen White might use the phrase "sanctified reason."

In this same connection, it is noteworthy that of the three great subjugations which Galatians 3:28 announces as being leveled in Christ (Jew/Gentile, slave/free, male/female), only the Jew/Gentile relationship was effectively addressed in the New Testament. Christians did not confront the slave/free issue until the nineteenth century and the male/female relationship is still being addressed today. But these are all casebook applications of larger principles, and such changes come about by thoughtful Christians in dialogue with each other and under the guidance of the Spirit, in other words, through "sanctified reason." The following quote illustrates a key way in which Ellen White used the phrase:

> Daily, hourly, we must be actuated by the principles of Bible truth,—righteousness, mercy, and the love of God. He who would have moral and intellectual power must draw from the divine source. At every point of decision inquire, "Is this the way of the Lord?" With your Bibles open before you, consult sanctified reason and a good conscience. Your heart must be moved, your soul touched, your reason and intellect awakened, by the Spirit of God; and then holy principles revealed in the word of God will give light to the soul.[30]

Romans 14. The thrust of this whole chapter is the call to allow room for diversity without causing another to stumble. Specific applications are made to holy days and to food: "Those who eat must not despise those who abstain," argues Paul, "and those who abstain must not pass judgment on those who eat."[31] This whole chapter, but especially verse 17, is the one that finally brought me over the line to a casebook approach when we were in Scotland: "For the kingdom of God is not food and drink but righteousness and peace and joy in the Holy Spirit." But it did not happen immediately. Even though the text is painfully clear to me now, I could not really believe it until I had prayed it through again and again. Finally, in the presence of one of God's dear children, I understood its truth and was able to put it into practice.

1 Corinthians 8; 9:19–23; 10:23–33. All these passages emphasize the importance of Christian adaptability. Yes, the Christian has liberty, "But take care that this liberty of yours does not somehow become a stumbling block to the weak." Paul's principle for his own behavior was: "I have become all things to all people, that I might by all means save some." And the principle applied to all Christians has far-reaching implications: "All things are lawful, but not all things are beneficial. All things are lawful, but not all things build up. Do not seek your own advantage, but that of the other." Paul is referring in the first instance to ritual and symbolic matters, rather than to matters of core morality or even matters of health. But, in a sense, for the Christian, the whole matter of recognizing another person's rights and privileges lies at the very heart of Christian morality. It is the living out of Jesus' second great command: "Love your neighbor as yourself."[32]

With these New Testament passages pointing the way, we can address the crucial issue of what changes in Scripture and what does not. Is there anything that is secure? There is indeed! But I know from personal experience, that for some who have approached Scripture and the writings of Ellen White from an all-or-nothing, codebook perspective, a casebook approach "feels" dangerous, relativistic, and reductionistic. Those are all words that devout believers have used in conversations with me as we have discussed the topic, often with great earnestness.

But before we look at the overall structure of "law" in Scripture, I would like to highlight three quotations from Ellen White which address the role of reason.

Ellen White on the Proper Role of Reason

The first quotation below addresses the role of reason in the educational process. It is found in Ellen White's first extended comment on education, coming relatively early in her experience (1872):

> **Using your own judgment (1872):** There are many families of children who appear to be well trained while under the training discipline; but when the system which has held them to set rules is broken up, they seem to be incapable of thinking, acting, or deciding for themselves. These children have been so long under iron rule, not allowed to think and act for themselves in those things in which it was highly proper that they should, that they have no confidence in themselves to move out upon their own judgment, having an opinion of their own. And when they go out from their parents to act for themselves, they are easily led by other's judgment in the wrong direction. They have not stability of character. *They have not been thrown upon their own judgment as fast and as far as practicable, and therefore their minds have not been properly developed and strengthened.* They have so long been absolutely controlled by their parents that they rely wholly upon them; their parents are mind and judgment for them.[33]

The next two quotations address the role of reason (and education!) in matters of health reform. The first quote comes from 1870 in one of Ellen White's early statements on health reform:

> **Treatment of disease to be based on knowledge (1870):** My voice shall be raised against novices undertaking to treat disease professedly according to the principles of health reform. God forbid that we should be the subjects for them to experiment upon! We are too few. It is altogether too inglorious a warfare for us to die in. God deliver us from such danger! We do not need such teachers and physicians. *Let those try to treat disease who know something about the human system.* The heavenly Physician was full of compassion. This spirit is needed by those who deal with the sick.

Some who undertake to become physicians are bigoted, selfish, and mulish. *You cannot teach them anything.* It may be they have never done anything worth doing. They may not have made life a success. They know nothing really worth knowing, and yet they have started up to practice the health reform. We cannot afford to let such persons kill off this one and that one. No; we cannot afford it![34]

Finally, a quotation from 1901 on the relationship of Ellen White's authority to one's decisions about health reform:

> **Ellen White herself not an authority:** If you have not got any better conviction—you won't eat meat because Sister White does not eat any—if I am the authority, I would not give a farthing for your health reform.[35]

The "Law Pyramid" and *Patriarchs and Prophets*

In the effort to construct a framework within which all God's commands could be placed, the significant source for me has been Ellen White's book, *Patriarchs and Prophets*. If Evangelical Christians focus on the condemning function of law, thus placing it in tension with grace, the Old Testament itself sees law as a gracious gift from God. Now, the violent punishments meted out in the Old Testament have tended to obscure this gracious aspect. Yet it is expounded at great length in Psalm 119 and described succinctly by Moses in Deuteronomy 4:5–8. After urging Israel to keep the statutes and ordinances given by God, Moses declares that the Israelites' commitment to divine instruction will be especially impressive to non-Israelite observers:

> This will show your wisdom and discernment to the peoples, who, when they hear all these statutes, will say, "Surely this great nation is a wise and discerning people!" For what other great nation has a god so near to it as the LORD our God is whenever we call to him? And what other great nation has statutes and ordinances as just as this entire law that I am setting before you today?[36]

To use a modern illustration, Moses sees law as a user-friendly owners manual. In the New Testament, Paul sees law more as a warranty agreement (which we can't possibly keep). Modern evangelicals, taking their cue from Paul's ambivalence about law in Romans 7 and from the explicit statement in Romans 3:20 that "through the law comes the knowledge of sin," too easily overlook the gracious intention behind law that comes through so clearly in the Old Testament. The following outline, with supporting Ellen White quotations—all except the first one from *Patriarchs and Prophets*— looks at law from the positive side. It is that perspective on law that is fully compatible with a casebook approach.

Ellen White on the Nature of Law
Adaptation and Restoration of the Ideal Law of Love

1. **Before sin entered heaven, the angels were virtually unaware of law** (*Thoughts From the Mount of Blessing*, p. 109): "In heaven, service is not rendered in the spirit of legality. When Satan rebelled against the law of Jehovah, the thought that there was a law came to the angels almost as an awakening to something unthought of. In their ministry the angels are not as servants, but as sons. There is perfect unity between them and their Creator. Obedience is to them no drudgery. Love for God makes their service a joy."

2. **Before sin on earth, the law was written on human hearts** (*Patriarchs and Prophets*, p. 363): "Adam and Eve, at their creation, had a knowledge of the law of God; they were acquainted with its claims upon them; its precepts were written upon their hearts. When man fell by transgression the law was not changed, but a remedial system was established to bring him back to obedience."

3. **Law adapted: Obedience would have made additional laws unnecessary** (*Patriarchs and Prophets*, p. 364): "If man had kept the law of God, as given to Adam after his fall, preserved by Noah, and observed by Abraham, there would have been no necessity for the ordinance of circumcision. And if the descendants of Abraham had kept the covenant, of which circumcision was a sign, they would never have been seduced into idolatry, nor would it have been necessary for them to suffer a life of bondage in Egypt; they would have kept God's law in mind, and there would have been no necessity for it to be proclaimed from Sinai, or engraved upon the tables of stone. And had the

people practiced the principles of the Ten Commandments, there would have been no need of the additional directions given to Moses."

4. **The Decalogue simply applies the principles of Jesus' two great commands** (*Patriarchs and Prophets,* p. 305): "The precepts of the Decalogue are adapted to all mankind and they were given for the instruction and government of all. Ten precepts, brief, comprehensive, and authoritative, cover the duty of man to God and to his fellowman; and all based upon the great fundamental principle of love. 'Thou shalt love the Lord thy God with all thy heart and with all thy soul and with all thy strength and with all thy mind and thy neighbor as thyself' (Luke 10:27). In the Ten Commandments, these principles are carried out in detail and made applicable to the condition and circumstances of man."

5. **Additional laws illumine the principles revealed in the Decalogue** (*Patriarchs and Prophets,* p. 310): "The minds of the people, blinded and debased by slavery and heathenism, were not prepared to appreciate fully the far-reaching principles of God's ten precepts. That the obligations of the Decalogue might be more fully understood and enforced, additional precepts were given, illustrating and applying the principles of the Ten Commandments."

6. **All these God-given laws were gracious in intent** (*Patriarchs and Prophets,* p. 311): "The object of all these regulations was stated: they proceeded from no exercise of arbitrary sovereignty; all were given for the good of Israel."

7. **God's ideal is simply the return to the full internalization of the law** (*Patriarchs and Prophets,* p. 372): "The same law that was engraved upon the tables of stone, is written by the Holy Spirit upon the tables of the heart."

The Essential Biblical Passages

The two most explicit biblical passages that describe the inner workings of this approach to law are Jeremiah 31:31–34 and Matthew 19:8.

Growing toward God: the law internalized (Jeremiah 31:31–34). "The days are surely coming, says the LORD, when I will make a new covenant with the house of Israel and the house of Judah. It will not be like the covenant that I made with their ancestors when I took them by the hand to bring them out of the land of Egypt— a covenant that they broke, though I was their husband, says the LORD. *But this is the covenant that I will make with the house of Israel after those days, says the LORD: I will put my law within them, and I will write it on their hearts; and I will be their God, and they shall be my people. No longer shall they teach one another, or say to each other, Know the LORD, for they shall all know me, from the least of them to the greatest, says the LORD;* for I will forgive their iniquity, and remember their sin no more" (emphasis supplied).

Falling away from God: the gracious gift of adapted law (Matthew 19:7, 8): "They said to him, Why then did Moses command us to give a certificate of dismissal and to divorce her? He said to them, *It was because you were so hard-hearted that Moses allowed you to divorce your wives, but from the beginning it was not so"* (emphasis supplied).

This approach to law is simple, beautiful, practical. As we draw nearer to God, the principles of His law become more and more a natural part of us, until living the law of love simply becomes second nature. That is Jeremiah's "new covenant." In the first instance, it has nothing at all to do with the coming of Jesus and it certainly is *not* a replacement of Old Testament law by a New Testament covenant centered in Jesus. The new covenant is actually a "renewal" of a healthy attitude towards God's will (law) and is a promise that applies with equal force in both testaments.

If, as we draw nearer to God, explicit, external laws become less necessary, the opposite is true when we are falling away from Him. The farther we fall, the more help we need to address our sinful condition. That is the truth offered by Jesus' statement on divorce in Matthew 19:8. In short, God is willing to adapt His will to our human needs. Such gracious adaptations are often the ones most likely to be dated and transcended as time goes on.

Finally, I should note that the principle of adaptation also provides us a way to address those laws and customs, especially in the Old Testament, that horrify us even though the Bible says they came from God. In that connection, however, a quotation from *Patriarchs and Prophets,* p. 515, is the only one from Ellen White that I know of that addresses that issue explicitly. Explaining why God chose to work with the "ancient custom of private vengeance," a custom requiring the next of kin to hunt down and kill any person who had killed a family member, even if the death had been accidental, Ellen White states: "This merciful provision was rendered necessary by the ancient custom of private vengeance." A few lines later she adds: "The Lord did not see fit to abolish this custom at that time, but He made provision to ensure the safety of those who should take life unintentionally."

I close this chapter with a question and an illustration. The question: Is there anything that doesn't change or move? Have we relativized everything? Let me answer that question with a good Adventist story.

Some Things Never Change

A few years ago while on sabbatical in Scotland, I was putting the finishing touches on my book *Inspiration: Hard Questions, Honest Answers*[37] when I happened by the office of a well-known Old Testament scholar and we chatted about our various projects. When he asked me what I was doing, I frankly told him that I was writing a book to help my students see more clearly what never changes in Scripture. I said I was sick and tired of seeing my students lose their faith when they discovered things in the Bible they didn't think were supposed to be there. Here's a brief summary of what I said:

The unchanging anchor in Scripture consists of the great principle of love, its more specific definition through Jesus' two great commands (love to God, love to your neighbor), and their even more specific application in the Ten Commandments. You can draw a double line around those laws, marking them off from everything else, for they never change. The rest of Scripture simply illustrates and applies them in particular times and places, an interpretation suggested by Jesus' summarizing comment on the two great commandments: "On these two commandments hang all the law and the prophets."[38]

While the two great commands are certainly enduring, the Ten Commandments represent an additional layer of stability. They, too, "hang" on the two great commands, but they never change. Draw your double line after the ten. Everything else in Scripture—all the laws and stories—"hang" on the two, illustrating how we are to understand and apply the fundamental principle of love, the two great commands, and the Ten Commandments in many and varied circumstances.

So, I thought to myself, *that's my good Adventist Bible study on the law.*

To my surprise, he replied without hesitation, "Of course that's where the Bible draws the double line. Look at Deuteronomy 4:13, 14."

Incredibly, our next few moments together still sounded like an old-fashioned Adventist Bible study on the law!

"Note the difference between verses 13 and 14," he said. "In verse 13, God is addressing Israel directly, not speaking through Moses. According to this text, God gave the people His covenant and described what He gave them as Ten Commandments. Furthermore, the text states that God Himself wrote the commandments on two stone tablets.

"But," my professor friend continued, "note the changes in verse 14. First, God is addressing Moses, not the people. Second, to Moses, He gave statutes and ordinances, not His covenant or the Ten Commandments.

"In short," he concluded, "you're quite right. The double line comes after the Ten Commandments. That's where the Bible itself puts it."

I was astounded that he would respond so spontaneously and so quickly with that solid "Adventist" exposition of the Bible. It's not just Adventist, of course. It's just a simple and straightforward reading of the Bible, a reading that should be evident to any honest person.

To make the "Bible study" complete, we would simply need to add two additional points. First, that the "statutes and ordinances" were written down by Moses in a book and placed *beside* the ark, not *in* the ark[39] and second, that the penalties for breaking the Ten Commandments are not included in the Decalogue itself but in the additional legislation, thus giving the Decalogue a more enduring quality.

I might note that penalties are much more likely to be shaped by time, place, and culture, and thus vary considerably, even in the Bible. In the Old Testament, for example, the additional Mosaic legislation assigns the death penalty to every one of the Ten Commandments except the last one (don't covet), an application matching the more violent needs of the violent people who had come out of Egypt.

Jesus, of course, coming to earth as God in the flesh, points us toward the nonviolent ideal, with the story of the woman taken in adultery being the most famous example: "Neither do I condemn you. Go your way, and from now on do not sin again."[40] Thus, in striking instances, Jesus could omit the penalty while still affirming the command as enduring.

Summary

In conclusion, I say with passion: Some things never change. God has spelled them out in Scripture with remarkable clarity—the one great principle of love, Jesus' two great commands, and the Ten Commandments. Everything else, all the "cases" He has ever given through inspiration and revelation, simply illustrate and apply these great principles, these great commands.

The capstone to this whole process of helping us know God's will is found in the revelation of God in Jesus Christ. He is the embodiment of God's law of love, the law pyramid in human flesh, so to speak. Through Him and through His example we learn best of all how we are to live.

But what is most important is the realization that all our good efforts to live out the law of love can never earn salvation. That is God's gift. And it is always a gift, never something that we earn by our efforts. Indeed, if we are really serious about living out God's law of love, we will discover the painful truth of the paradox noted in Ellen White's *Steps to Christ*: "The closer you come to Jesus, the more faulty you will appear in your own eyes; for your vision will be clearer, and your imperfections will be seen in broad and distinct contrast to His perfect nature."[41]

That is when we stand side-by-side with Brother Paul, and for all our talk about the "good news" version of law, we cry out with him: "Wretched man that I am! Who will rescue me from this body of death?"[42]

But Paul didn't stop with wretchedness. Nor should we. We must move on with him from the anguish of Romans 7 to the exuberance of Romans 8: "There is therefore now no condemnation for those who are in Christ Jesus."[43]

Yes, the law is good news. It is our anchor, protecting us from a host of evils and helping us to know what is good. But if you will pardon the mixed metaphor, we will never go anywhere at all if all we have is an anchor. The law is indeed our anchor, but Jesus is the wind in our sails. He is our strength, our power, our motivation. And it is because of Jesus that we can say with Paul:

> I am convinced that neither death, nor life, nor angels nor rulers, nor things present, nor things to come, nor powers, nor height, nor depth, nor anything else in all creation, will be able to separate us from the love of God in Christ Jesus our Lord.—Romans 8:38, 39.

So, with a secure anchor (the law) and with the wind in our sails (Jesus) we can move to the next chapter where we will explore with specific illustrations from the Bible and from the writings of Ellen White, what it means to move from fear to joy, from an emphasis on God's power to an emphasis on His goodness. Both His power and His goodness are manifestations of His love, to be sure. But it is an appreciation of His goodness that brings true joy to the heart.

---

[1] 1 Timothy 2:12.
[2] See Daniel 6:8, 12; Esther 8:8.
[3] Genesis 27:33.
[4] Joshua 9:18.
[5] Joshua 9:15, 18, 19; 2 Samuel 21:6, 9.
[6] Judges 21:22.
[7] Genesis 3:9, 10.
[8] Genesis 4:23.
[9] Known as the *lex talionis,* the law of revenge: Exodus 21:23, 24. In the Sermon on the Mount, Jesus takes the next step, internalizing the ideal with the command to go the second mile and turn the other cheek (Matthew 5:38–42).
[10] Exodus 32:27.
[11] Joshua 1:18.
[12] Genesis 22:12–14.
[13] Exodus 13:1–16.
[14] 2 Kings 3:27.
[15] 2 Kings 21:6.

[16] Micah 6:7.

[17] Judges 21:22.

[18] 1 Samuel 14:45.

[19] Proverbs 26:4, 5.

[20] *The Desire of Ages,* p. 530 (1898).

[21] Matthew 21:12–17.

[22] Jeremiah 31:34.

[23] Lloyd M. Graham, *Deceptions and Myths of the Bible* (New York, N.Y.: Carol Publishing Group, 1995 [1975]).

[24] "Love to man is the earthward manifestation of the love of God. It was to implant this love, to make us children of one family, that the king of glory became one with us. And when His parting words are fulfilled, Love one another, as I have loved you (John 15:12); when we love the world as He has loved it, then for us His mission is accomplished. We are fitted for heaven; for we have heaven in our hearts."—*The Desire of Ages,* p. 641 (1898).

[25] Isaiah 58:6.

[26] See, for example, Isaiah 1:11–17; Amos 5:18–27; Jeremiah 7:1–15, 21–26.

[27] Healing of the man with the withered hand: Matthew 12:9–14; Mark 3:1–6; Luke 6:6–11; healing of the stooped woman: Luke 13:10–17; healing of the man with dropsy: Luke 14:1–6; healing of the man at the pool: John 5; healing of the man born blind: John 9. For commentary on these Sabbath miracles see John C. Brunt, *A Day for Healing* (Washington, D.C.: Review and Herald, 1981).

[28] Acts 15:11.

[29] Acts 15:28.

[30] *The Review and Herald,* February 7, 1893, para. 13.

[31] Romans 14:3.

[32] 1 Corinthians 8:9; 9:22; 10:23, 24; Matthew 22:39.

[33] *Testimonies for the Church,* vol. 3, pp. 132, 133 (1872), emphasis supplied.

[34] *Testimonies for the Church,* vol. 2, p. 375 (1870), emphasis supplied.

[35] Manuscript Release #624: Ms. 43a, 1901, p. 13. ("Talk of Mrs. E. G. White, Before Representative Brethren, in the [Battle Creek] College Library, April 1, 1901.) *Manuscript Releases,* vol. 8, p. 350 (1990), released June 21, 1978.

[36] Deuteronomy 4:6–8.

[37] Alden Thompson, *Inspiration: Hard Questions, Honest Answers* (Hagerstown: Review and Herald, 1991).

[38] Matthew 22:40.

[39] Deuteronomy 31:24–26.

[40] John 8:11, NRSV.

[41] *Steps to Christ,* pp. 64, 65.

[42] Romans 7:24.

[43] Romans 8:1.

CHAPTER 10

From Fear to Joy:
The Illustrations

Some time ago I came across a tantalizing quote in one of George Knight's excellent little books on Ellen White.[1] Knight, Professor of Church History at the Seventh-day Adventist Theological Seminary at Andrews University, and I are good friends. He has been supportive of my writings on inspiration, even contributing a cover quote for *Inspiration: Hard Questions, Honest Answers*.[2] But he has not been particularly enthusiastic about my "growth" model for approaching Scripture and the life and writings of Ellen White. And it's not because we haven't talked about it, even at length.

So it was with particular interest that I read this paragraph, published in his 1996 book, *Meeting Ellen White*:

> One of the most forceful illustrations of the centrality of God's love in Ellen White's writings is that the phrase "God is love" provides the first three words in the first volume of the Conflict of the Ages Series (*Patriarchs and Prophets*) and the last three words of the series' final volume (*The Great Controversy*).[3]

Intrigued by the quote, I went to Ellen White's earliest published version of the "great controversy" story, *Spiritual Gifts, volume 1* (1858). In that little volume, the entire story from "The Fall of Man" to "The Second Death" is covered in just 202 small pages,[4] rather more concise than the some 3,700 full-size pages of the five-volume Conflict series.

I carefully read through the entire story, making note of every use of the word "love" and its derivatives. I found it applied frequently to Christ, but not once to the Father. Not quite ready yet to trust my own eye, I went to the official disk of Ellen White publications and ran a search for "God is love" in volume 1 of *Spiritual Gifts*. The search program would also list any occurrences of the phrase "God of love." My computer went to work and shortly popped the following message on the screen: "Your last search retrieved no records."

When I called up Knight and shared with him my discovery, there was a pause at the other end. Then he said, "Thompson, you may be on to something."

I think so. And the purpose of this chapter is to share some of the evidence to show that Ellen White moved from fear to joy in her experience, from an emphasis on God's power to an emphasis on His love.

[handwritten margin note: Is this because EGW moved or because God moved?]

Avoiding the Contrasts

The contrasting illustrations noted in this chapter don't often appear in books written by and for devout believers and for several reasons. First, when critics point to "contradictions" as an argument against Scripture, believers easily turn defensive and simply resist seeing them. Instead of denying the "contradictions," however, I believe we should seize the initiative and demonstrate that the contrasting passages are the solution, not the problem.

A second reason why these comparisons and contrasts seldom appear in print is that we who believe are often highly selective in what we see in "inspired" writings. From my work in classroom and church, I have observed four basic reactions to the "violence" found in parts of the Bible. You can choose your own tendency from the following:

1. **Idolize the violence.** This is a minority response. But there are some who are eager to point to God's heavy hand as the solution to all the problems in the church and the world.

2. **Idealize the stories.** This is a popular impulse among believers. Almost all children's Bible stories smooth over the difficult parts. Uncle Arthur, Uncle Dan and Aunt Sue, and Ellen White all do it. And so do the Bible writers. Chronicles idealizes the stories of Samuel-Kings, omitting, for example, all the ugly bits about David and Solomon, and Hebrews 11 is a strictly good-news version of some startling Old Testament stories—Sarah laughs at God in Gen-

esis, but not in Hebrews 11. Jack Blanco's *Clear Word* represents a thorough-going application of the idealizing impulse.

3. **Avoid or ignore the troublesome.** The tendency to avoid or ignore the harsh and troublesome may be as strong as the tendency to idealize. And the impulse is quite understandable. When we turn to Scripture for solace, encouragement, and inspiration, we are not likely to seek out that which is unsettling and troubling, much less that which horrifies us.

4. **Realism.** This is my preferred option, though I don't argue that we should give all Scripture equal billing. The Gospels, for example, are more likely to be helpful than the book of Judges. But I do believe we should be honest with Scripture. All of it. And I believe we can discover good reasons why Scripture is the way it is rather than the way we wish it were. I apply the same principles to the writings of Ellen White.

Now, even though I have identified "realism" as my preferred option, I argue in the next chapter that the other perspectives are also important to have in the church. It would be dangerous to believe that everyone in the church should think like I do. Indeed, in a sense, any one of us could be a danger to the church! The writings of Ellen White have helped me come to this conclusion. But the attempt to *explain* "diversity" is for the next chapter. Here I *illustrate* it. Or, to put it another way, in the next chapter, I will attempt to explain why some thoughtful and devout believers don't like this explanation.

1. Illustrations From the Bible

In most of the illustrations which follow (especially in the writings of Ellen White in the next section), a key determining factor (and often the key difference) is the method of motivation. Typically fear is a reaction to *awe* God's power, joy a response to His goodness. In some instances, however, a glimpse of God's goodness can trigger a reaction of fear, even terror. That's what happened to Peter after the miraculous harvest of fish: "Depart from me, for I am a sinful man, O Lord."[5] In general, however, we are looking at the difference between threats and bribes (to use rather crass language),

What about if you are running away

From Fear to Joy: The Illustrations • 139

between negative and positive motivation. And Scripture is clear that God is willing to use both—and everything in between. At the risk of over-generalizing, we could say that the Old Testament is heavy on the negative, while the New Testament stresses the positive. To be sure, there are striking examples of both in both testaments. One of the best biblical illustrations of the negative and the positive being laid side-by-side is Paul's exclamation to the Corinthians: "What would you prefer? Am I to come to you with a stick, or with love in a spirit of gentleness?"[6] Matthew records Jesus' variation on that theme, perhaps a popular street jingle which Jesus had picked up: "We played the flute for you [the positive], and you did not dance; we wailed [the negative], and you did not mourn."[7]

In short, God does not limit Himself to the "ideal" method. He is the ultimate pragmatist and will use what works. The apostle Paul is just following the divine example when he exclaims: "To the weak I became weak, so that I might win the weak. I have become all things to all people that I might by all means save some."[8]

A. David's Census: God or Satan?

God as active agent: "Again the anger of the LORD was kindled against Israel, and he incited David against them, saying, 'Go, count the people of Israel and Judah' " (2 Samuel 24:1).

Satan as active agent: "Satan stood up against Israel, and incited David to count the people of Israel" (1 Chronicles 21:1).

Some are tempted to consider the Chronicles passage as true, but the Samuel passage as false because God is portrayed as the active agent of evil. I believe they both represent "truth" as adapted to particular human needs and circumstances. Indeed, I am convinced that recognizing the shift here from God to Satan as the active agent of evil is important for understanding the "violent" Old Testament God, a topic already addressed in chapter 7.

B. Retaliate or Turn the Other Cheek?

Retaliate: "You shall give life for life, eye for eye, tooth for tooth, hand for hand, foot for foot, burn for burn, wound for wound, stripe for stripe" (Exodus 21:23–25).

Turn the other cheek: "You have heard that it was said, 'An eye for an eye and a tooth for a tooth.' But I say to you, Do not resist an evildoer. But if anyone strikes you on the right cheek, turn the other also" (Matthew 5:38, 39).

At the superficial level, this comparison can be misleading. The clear scholarly consensus is that the Old Testament eye-for-eye passages belong in a legal context and were originally intended to limit revenge, not encourage it. The deeply entrenched custom of blood vengeance, for which the cities of refuge were a partial remedy,[9] represents a violent and undisciplined extension of the eye-for-eye principle. But Jesus' interpretation of God's "ideal" could only apply to individuals who choose the high standard for themselves. It could never serve as the basis for civil law. Still, Jesus' comments call attention to the popular (mis)understanding of what the Old Testament allowed.

C. Hate or Love Your Enemies?

Hate your enemies: "Do I not hate those who hate you, O Lord? And do I not loathe those who rise up against you? I hate them with perfect hatred; I count them my enemies" (Psalm 139:21, 22).

Love your enemies: "You have heard that it was said, 'You shall love your neighbor and hate your enemy.' But I say to you, love your enemies and pray for those who persecute you" (Matthew 5:43, 44).

Jesus' quotation of the "tradition" is intriguing, for the command to "hate your enemy" is nowhere found in the Old Testament. "You shall love your neighbor," of course, is a quotation from Leviticus 19:18. And the preceding lines command, "Do not hate your brother in your heart. . . . Do not seek revenge or bear a grudge against one of your people."[10] But those are all in-house relations. Exodus 23:4, 5 commands compassion towards an enemy's ox or ass. But the focus is still on the enemy's animals, not on the enemy himself.

What really sets the tone for the "violent" reputation of the Old Testament, however, are the divine commands to obliterate national enemies, such as the Amalekites in 1 Samuel 15 and the vengeful attitudes toward one's enemies as quoted in Psalm 139 above and in numerous other psalms as well.[11] Together, these passages give the impression that it was entirely appropriate to hate one's enemies.

Jesus confronted head on that popular impression, not only commanding His followers to love their enemies but also demonstrating on the cross how to ask forgiveness for them.[12] And Jesus was not just teaching in-house love; the Syro-Phoenician woman, the Gadarene demoniac, the Samaritan woman at the well, and the good Samaritan himself could all testify that Jesus' love was all-encompassing. Jesus had found the Suffering Servant song of Isaiah 53 (in the Old Testament, even!) and made it the cornerstone of His ministry.

D. Salvation: Hard or Easy?

Hard: The rich young ruler: " 'There is still one thing lacking. Sell all that you own and distribute the money to the poor, and you will have treasure in heaven; then come, follow me.' " (Luke 18:22).

Easy: The Philippian jailer: " 'Sirs, what must I do to be saved?' They answered, 'Believe on the Lord Jesus, and you will be saved, you and your household' " (Acts 16:30, 31).

If one surveys all the "salvation" conversations in the New Testament, one discovers a stunning variety of responses. Even the wealthy are treated quite differently. For example, the rich young ruler was asked to give up everything,[13] but Zacchaeus voluntarily gave up half his goods,[14] and Scripture records no rebuke. There is no simple formula which applies in all cases.

E. Decisive Exclusion or Patient Inclusion?

Drive them out: "Now I am writing to you not to associate with anyone who bears the name of brother or sister who is sexually immoral or greedy, or is an idolater, reviler, drunkard, or robber. Do not even eat with such a one. . . . Drive out the wicked person from among you" (1 Corinthians 5:11, 13).

Love them in: "Love is patient; love is kind; love is not envious or boastful or arrogant or rude. It does not insist on its own way; it is not irritable or resentful" (1 Corinthians 13:4, 5).

The appearance of these two contrasting passages in the same letter from the same author makes them particularly striking. Note that 1 Corinthians 5:11 even puts the "greedy" on the forbidden list. Was Paul as "patient and kind" as he admonished the Corinthians to be in chapter 13? Apparently not.

2. Illustrations From Ellen White

While the biblical examples cited above do not tidily follow an Old Testament/New Testament division, there is a general contrast between the Testaments, with Jesus modeling the more gentle and positive motivation. There are notable exceptions, however, with positive in the Old and negative in the New.

A similar pattern can be traced in the writings of Ellen White, with a general contrast between "early" and "late," or put more accurately, a steady movement toward the positive. But in her experience, too, one can find good examples of the positive in her early years and instances of the negative in her later years.

Most of the following illustrations are taken from Ellen White's three successive commentary series: *Spiritual Gifts* (1858–1864), *Spirit of Prophecy* (1870–1884), and Conflict of the Ages (1890–1917), thus providing insights into Ellen White's thinking at three points in her experience at roughly twenty-year intervals.

A. John the Baptist's Simple Life: Burdensome or Joyous?

Ellen White told the story of John the Baptist in all three of her commentary series. Having grown up with the view of John as found in *The Desire of Ages,* her latest edition of the story (1898), I was startled to discover the tone of the earlier editions—then amazed as I noted the pattern:

> **1858:** "John's life was without pleasure. It was sorrowful and self-denying."—*Spiritual Gifts,* vol. 1, p. 29.
>
> **1877:** "John's life, with the exception of the joy he experienced in witnessing the success of his mission, was without pleasure." —*Spirit of Prophecy,* vol. 2, p. 69.

1897: "John enjoyed his life of simplicity and retirement." —*The Youth's Instructor,* January 7, 1897.

1898: "Aside from the joy that John found in his mission, his life had been one of sorrow."—*The Desire of Ages,* p. 220.

In all of the accounts, John's simple life remains constant. The difference is whether he experienced his simple life as a burden or as a joy. Scripture is silent on the question, leaving Ellen White the opportunity to interpret the story in terms of her own experience. When simplicity is experienced as a sacrifice demanded by an austere God, it can be practiced, though it is likely to be a joyless experience. By contrast, when simplicity is a loving response to a gracious God, the very same life style can be transformed from a burden into a joy.

Note the progressive softening of tone with each successive edition. In the first account, John's life is without a glimmer of joy; in the second, he at least has good times at work; finally, his whole experience is transformed, and he enjoys his life of simplicity. As one of my students quipped when I first presented these quotes in class, "You mean the more Ellen White enjoyed her experience in the Lord, the more John the Baptist enjoyed his." Exactly. And from a literary perspective, it is interesting to sense the transformation of tone in *The Desire of Ages* simply by the omission of the phrase, "without pleasure."

B. Family Love: Rival of Divine Love or Illustration of Divine Love?

As noted in chapter 9, in the larger religious scene (perhaps seen more clearly outside the Adventist Church), devout "conservatives" who worship a more authoritarian God, tend to focus on the vertical relationship (obedience to God), while neglecting or even running rough-shod over horizontal relationships (love for one's neighbor). One of the most terrifying illustrations of that impulse is the 9/11 attack by terrorists who believed they were being faithful to their God.

By contrast, "liberals" tend to emphasize horizontal relationships. Lloyd Graham's quote, cited earlier, illustrates that position in its starkest form when he calls for breaking the "scriptural tyranny" "so that we may devote our time to man instead of God and to civilizing ourselves instead of saving our souls that were never lost."[15] In short, the nonbelieving author might even agree with Jesus' second great command (love to neighbor), but has no time at all for the first one (love to God).

The following quotes illustrate how Ellen White moved from the more conservative (authoritarian) position toward a more liberal stance, but in such a way that she integrates the two positions into a harmonious whole. The differing perspectives come in the two editions of her story of the wedding at Cana, recorded in Scripture in John 2. The key lines come in her interpretation of Jesus' response to His mother: "Woman, what concern is that to you and to me? My hour has not yet come."[16]

> **Rebuking His mother (1877):** "In rebuking his mother, Jesus also rebukes a large class who have an idolatrous love for their family, and allow the ties of relationship to draw them from the service of God. Human love is a sacred attribute; but should not be allowed to mar our religious experience, or draw our hearts from God."—*Spirit of Prophecy,* vol. 2, pp. 101, 102.
>
> **Respecting His mother (1898):** "This answer, abrupt as it seems to us, expressed no coldness or discourtesy. The Saviour's form of address to his mother was in accordance with Oriental custom. It was used toward persons to whom it was desired to show respect."—*The Desire of Ages,* p. 146.

The context of these two quotations further underscores the contrast between them. In the 1877 quote, the tone of rebuke continues on in the next paragraph: "But Mary, in the pride of her heart, longed to see him prove to the company that he was really the honored of God."[17] The parallel is not precise, but the 1898 quote is preceded by words that affirm Mary's *natural* pride: "Yet she would have been more than human if there had not mingled with this holy joy a trace of the fond mother's natural pride."[18] Another quote further on in *The Desire of Ages,* one already cited earlier, reveals how Ellen White has resolved the tension between the human and the divine, rather than seeing them as being in tension with each other:

Love to man is the earthward manifestation of the love of God. It was to implant this love, to make us children of one family, that the King of glory became one with us. And when His parting words are fulfilled, 'Love one another, as I have loved you' (John 15:12); when we love the world as He has loved it, then for us His mission is accomplished. We are fitted for heaven; for we have heaven in our hearts.[19]

C. God's Love for Bad Children

Turning from Ellen White's interpretations of Scripture to practical applications, one of the more startling contrasts is how Ellen White relates God's love to those who do not obey Him. The first quote is from a letter to her children, the second is from an article in *Signs of the Times,* some thirty years later.

God does not love bad children (1860): "The Lord loves those little children who try to do right, and He has promised that they shall be in His kingdom. But wicked children God does not love. . . . When you feel tempted to speak impatient and fretful, remember the Lord sees you, and will not love you if you do wrong."[20]

God loves bad children (1892): "Do not teach your children that God does not love them when they do wrong; teach them that He loves them so that it grieves His tender Spirit to see them in transgression."[21]

Some might be tempted to solve the "contradiction" by noting that the earlier quote was in a letter to Ellen White's children, thus not carrying the same "inspired" clout as material published for a wider audience. But exactly the same view is found in a "published" testimony from 1856: "God will have a people separate and distinct from the world. And as soon as any have a desire to imitate the fashions of the world, that they do not immediately subdue, just so soon God ceases to acknowledge them as His children."—*Testimonies for the Church,* vol. 1, p. 137 (1856).

An interesting personal story lies behind this particular cluster of quotations dealing with God's love for those not doing right. In chapter 3, I briefly mentioned my failed early attempts at reading *Testimonies for the Church.* I don't remember any particular quotations that drove me away. It was more just the general tenor, as I recall. I seriously doubt if I got as far as page 137.

But when the fear-to-love model fell into place as a result of my study of Scripture, I could afford to see even the most vivid quotes without flinching—well, to be perfectly honest, I probably still flinched, but I no longer had to bracket the tough stuff as not being the result of "inspiration." Ellen White had convinced me that "God and heaven alone are infallible"[22] and that not everything given by inspiration is a direct reflection of God in His absolute goodness and purity.

In any event, I had quoted this passage in the five-part "Sinai to Golgotha" series published in the *Adventist Review* in December 1982. Immediately following this vivid "fashions" quote from *Testimonies for the Church,* vol. 1, p. 137, I added the following comment in my original manuscript:

> I reflected on the contrast represented by the children's song I had recently heard: "Jesus loves me when I'm good, when I do the things I should. Jesus loves me when I'm bad, even though it makes him sad." Young Ellen would have liked to sing that song, but she couldn't. She was still too close to Sinai.

Even though we had negotiated virtually everything else in the article, the editors replaced that quote at the last minute because one of their staff members felt I was being inappropriately critical of Ellen White. I can understand that very well—now, better than I did then. If one is a devout believer, the "negative" evidence is likely to simply disappear into the woods unless one has a model in which it all makes sense. Our relationship with God is too precious to let it be jeopardized by a "problem" here or a "problem" there.

But perhaps the more vivid memory connected with this quotation came in a telephone conversation with an Adventist woman who was attending my public presentations of the Sinai-Golgotha material, given over selected weekends in the autumn of 1981. After I had referred to the vivid "fashions" quotation cited above, she called up with a query/comment. This is how the conversation went:

"Did you know that Ellen White wrote a letter to her children in which she said that God would not love them if they are bad?" she asked.

"She did?" I responded.

"And did you know that it was published in the *Primary Treasure* a few years ago?"

"It was?" I said, my interest increasing every moment.

I asked her immediately if she knew the date of the letter. She couldn't remember.

"I'm guessing that it was 1859 or 1860," I said. And when she sent the copies to me, that was exactly the date of the letter—1860. All that is one of the reasons why I feel so keenly about dating Ellen White quotations—and why it is so important to see biblical material in its proper historical context. Dates do make a difference.

In all of the above comparisons, the harsher and more rigorous view comes from Ellen White's earlier writings. That would explain why the more rigorous self-supporting Adventist movements usually prefer the early writings of Ellen White, while the more gentle mainstream Adventists prefer the later writings. The more intense conservatives will even argue that the later writings were not inspired, but were shaped by Ellen White's secretaries. Ironically, liberal Adventists who may be inclined toward cynicism often suggest that the real Ellen White was in fact harsh and rigid, it was the secretaries who were nice and gentle. The mainstream church typically has ignored the differences in time and place, which often results in some very strange juxtapositions.

Is there common ground? I believe so. In all of the above instances, one sees a movement *away* from external motivation and an emphasis on God's power, and a movement *toward* internal motivation and an emphasis on God's goodness. To use more modern language, it is the movement from fearful threats to joyous invitations (Paul's "stick" vs. "love in a spirit of gentleness" in 1 Corinthians 4:21), en route to a completely spontaneous love response as described by Jeremiah: "No longer shall they teach one another or say to each other 'Know the Lord,' for they shall all know me, from the least of them to the greatest, says the LORD, for I will forgive their iniquity and remember their sin no more."[23]

If one is simply looking for inspired writers to provide the correct "information," one is tempted to ask which one is right and jettison the rest. That's the wrong question. Here is an illustration of God's use of the prophet to lead the people. We need all the evidence to make the story complete, just as one needs the more violent Old Testament in order to make the New Testament story complete. One cannot pick and choose.

Basking in the Full Light of the Father's Love

If, as I have tried to show in this chapter, God was moving Ellen White from fear to joy in her experience with Him, a fine capstone and conclusion to this chapter is provided by a quotation found in both *Steps to Christ* (1892) and *The Desire of Ages* (1898), but missing completely from the earlier accounts in *Spiritual Gifts* (1858) and *Spirit of Prophecy*, vol. 4 (1878). Building on John 10:17 (which she quotes), Ellen White's confidence in the Father's love for sinners has grown to the point that she can actually say that the Father's love for His fallen creation is so great that when the Son gave His life for us, the Father loved the Son even more because of it. I suspect Ellen White realized the inadequacy of language to get her point across. But the sentiment is still powerful and shows that Ellen White has truly escaped from the flames and has discovered true joy in the Lord:

> "Therefore doth My Father love Me, because I lay down My life, that I might take it again" [John 10:17]. That is, My Father has so loved you, that He even loves Me more for giving My life to redeem you. In becoming your substitute and surety, by surrendering My life, by taking your liabilities, your transgressions, I am endeared to My Father.[24]

---

[1] George R. Knight, *Meeting Ellen White* (1996); *Reading Ellen White* (1997); *Ellen White's World* (1998); *Walking with Ellen White* (1999). All are published by Review and Herald Publishing Association.

[2] Alden Thompson, *Inspiration: Hard Questions, Honest Answers* (Hagerstown, Md.: Review and Herald, 1991). The cover quote: "It will be a bombshell to many since it describes difficulties

faced by Bible readers. . . . It kept me awake and on the edge of my chair."—George R. Knight, professor of church history, Seventh-day Adventist Theological Seminary.

[3] Knight, *Meeting Ellen White,* p. 110.

[4] Ellen White, *Spiritual Gifts: The Great Controversy Between Christ and His Angels and Satan and His Angels,* vol. 1 (Battle Creek, 1858; reprint: Hagerstown, Md.: Review and Herald, 1945), pp. 17–219.

[5] Luke 5:8.

[6] 1 Corinthians 4:21.

[7] Matthew 11:17.

[8] 1 Corinthians 9:22.

[9] Cf. Numbers 35:9–28.

[10] Leviticus 19:17, 18, NIV.

[11] For example: Psalms 18:37–42; 69:22–28; 137.

[12] Luke 23:34.

[13] Luke 18:18–23.

[14] Luke 19:8.

[15] Lloyd M. Graham, *Deceptions and Myths of the Bible* (New York, N.Y.: Carol Publishing Group, 1995 [1975]).

[16] John 2:4.

[17] *Spirit of Prophecy,* vol. 2, p. 102 (1878).

[18] *The Desire of Ages,* p. 145 (1898).

[19] *Ibid.,* p. 641 (1898).

[20] Ellen White letter to her children, March 14, 1860, in *An Appeal to the Youth: Funeral Address of Henery M. White* (Battle Creek: Mich.: Steam Press, 1864), pp. 61–63.

[21] *Signs of the Times,* February, 15, 1892.

[22] *Selected Messages,* Book 1, p. 37 (1892).

[23] Jeremiah 31:33, 34.

[24] *Steps to Christ,* p. 14 (1892); *The Desire of Ages,* pp. 483, 484 (1898).

CHAPTER 11

Hopes and Fears

In chapter 3, I briefly described the powerful experience that was mine in the spring of 1979 when I taught Adventist history for the first time. I had just completed reading through all nine volumes of the *Testimonies for the Church,* a key element, I believe. But given all the complex factors that go into the making of an "exciting" class, I sensed that somehow God's Spirit had done wondrous things in bringing onto common ground an amazingly diverse college class of eighty students. Here, from chapter 3, is the description of the impact that experience had on me:

> In that class I glimpsed something that I sensed could work for the entire Adventist family. The dream which took on flesh and blood in that classroom has been a driving force in my life ever since. That is the experience I want for my church. And in a very real sense, that's why I'm writing this book.

In this final chapter, I address some crucial questions that inevitably arise in the light of my conclusion that God guided Ellen White in a growing experience, gradually moving her out of, and away from, the devastating effects of her early belief in an eternally burning hell. In short, the Spirit led her from an early emphasis on God's power (fear), to a deeper appreciation of His goodness (joy). I address those questions against the backdrop of some of my own experiences in the last twenty-five years. The tumultuous events in Adventism during that time have only deepened my convictions that the basic fear-to-joy model has a great deal to offer the church.[1]

Actually, the increasing evidence of diversity in Adventism undergirds my convictions all the more, even while I am discovering diverse views on

Ellen White. In Battle Creek, Michigan, for example, at the 2002 Conference on Ellen White and Adventist History, I observed some remarkably different perspectives on Ellen White's *Testimonies for the Church,* but in quite unexpected places. At that conference I had met Don McMahon, an Adventist physician from Australia, who has been exploring the "development" of Ellen White's understanding of health reform. With our presentations scheduled back-to-back, it was exciting and encouraging to see how closely his conclusions about Ellen White's development paralleled my own. Even though his focus was on Ellen White's developing understanding of health science and mine was on her developing understanding of God, we both had come to remarkably similar conclusions about the nature of her development and the reasons for it. In both cases, our research had confirmed our convictions that God was working through Ellen White in a special way, one that set her apart from her contemporaries in Adventism as God's special messenger. What was even more striking was that his starting point was from a liberal Adventism which virtually ignored Ellen White and mine was from a conservative Adventism which took Ellen White's counsel very seriously indeed. We have continued to have productive conversations.

At the same conference, however, I was startled to discover some widely differing perspectives on Ellen White's writings, even among devout academics, all of whom deeply appreciate her ministry in one way or another. With reference to *Testimonies for the Church,* for example, I had turned away from them in my teen years without really knowing why, but rediscovered them as an adult, finding them to be a rich resource for confirming two key elements in my understanding of how God works with human beings—the fear-to-joy model and a casebook approach to God-given law/counsel. A second brother in the faith, however, was actually drawn to *Testimonies for the Church* in his teen years, reading through the entire set as a non-Adventist high school student—but, I might add, without developing any enthusiasm for a casebook approach. Finally, a third brother quietly commented to me that he didn't think anyone should read *Testimonies for the Church* today. Amazing: three deeply committed Adventists, enthusiastic participants at the same Ellen White Conference, but differing widely in their views of her *Testimonies for the Church.*

Before we turn specifically to the major questions which the fear-to-joy model raises, I want to briefly elaborate on some of my own personal experiences that have significantly shaped my thinking since teaching that landmark class in Adventist history in the spring of 1979.

Opening Up to Diversity: My Own Experience

Several intense personal and corporate experiences have opened my own eyes to the reality of diversity within the church. Reflecting on these experiences in the light of Scripture and the writings of Ellen White, I see an increasingly urgent need, not just to recognize and/or tolerate diversity in the life and thinking of the church, but to embrace it as a strength. We certainly should *not* shun it as a weakness or a danger. In short, I am convinced that diversity is the true path to unity, and, when properly understood, can protect us from the dangers of relativism.

In addition to the dramatic effect that our stays in Scotland have had on my life and thinking, the following experiences have also been significant.

Discovering Differences in Temperament (Germany)

Intense. That's the best word to describe our year in Germany where I served as an exchange teacher at Marienhöhe Seminary in 1980-81. In many ways, it was a foolhardy thing to attempt—highly rewarding, but still foolhardy.

We had dreamed up the idea of an exchange after I finished my doctoral studies. Having suffered through miserably long chunks of scholarly German during my doctoral program, I didn't want all that pain to go for nought. I knew I wouldn't have the resolve to keep my German alive after we returned to the States. But if I taught in German for a year, the language might stick, and we might even be able to afford the venture.

The president at Marienhöhe Seminary, Heinz Henning, was definitely interested in the idea of an exchange, tenaciously so, and that proved important. A one-time event with no precedents means plenty of red tape. But the exchange finally happened, some four years and fifty-two pieces of correspondence after our first inquiry.

In several ways our stay in Germany helped shape my thinking toward Ellen White (and toward Scripture). But two words capture the dominant elements: "temperament" and "authority." What Wanda and I noticed immediately—and the impression deepened as the year progressed—was the incredible energy the Germans pour into almost everything. Wanda even began a list of all the things a German *Hausfrau* does simply by raw energy, rather than looking for American-style shortcuts.

On the biblical and theological front, that enormous energy tends to push to extremes. Some of the most vocal critics of the Bible (and of Ellen White) are of Germanic stock. Similarly, some of the most tenacious defenders of the authority of the Bible spring from the same family tree. And, not infrequently, a powerful defender can turn a hundred and eighty degrees and become an outspoken critic.

The tension between the more logical rationalist and the more emotional pietist is also noteworthy. More typically, the rationalist is the critic of faith and the pietist the defender, but in Germanic circles, even the most intense pietist will generally employ powerful rationalist arguments in defense of the faith.

That intensity of temperament also has a bearing on attitudes towards authority. Ever since World War I, the German Adventist community has been divided between the mainstream Adventists who are more willing to obey civil authority and accommodate to the dominant culture, and the smaller, but intense "Reform Movement" which is more separatist and sectarian in nature and much more tenaciously committed to the specific counsels of Ellen White. The Reform Movement has tended to separate itself not only from the dominant secular culture, but also from mainstream denominational leadership, which, it claims, has often compromised the faith in its willingness to accommodate to state and culture.

Interestingly enough, when we were in Germany, the German translation of *Messages to Young People* (1938) (*Ruf an die Jugend* [1951]) was out of print. At that time, mainstream denominational leadership in Germany was resisting the call from the more conservative voices in the church to bring it back into print. Except for the minority who are sympathetic to the Reform Movement, German Adventists are less inclined than mainstream American Adventists to view Ellen White as "authoritative." Admittedly, however, the furor over Ellen White's use of sources was just beginning to erupt when we were there. And since the publication of Walter Rea's *The*

White Lie (1982), attitudes on both sides of the Atlantic have been in considerable flux.

Of the various experiences that shaped us during our year in Germany, probably the most memorable had to do with reactions to the "good news" (user-friendly owner's manual) approach to law/counsel as discussed in chapter 9.[2] When I presented that more positive approach to law—it almost sounds like natural law—to my students in Germany, I quite misread their reaction. Since I was brand new on German soil, I subconsciously read their body language as if they were American students, concluding, therefore, that the material was so familiar as to be boring. So I moved on rather more quickly than I should have, assuming that they fully understood what I was saying. That was in August. Six months later, in February, a very bright student in the class asked a question that suddenly turned on the lights for me. What I thought they had fully understood to the point of boredom, they were only beginning to grasp six months later. Their body language meant puzzlement, not boredom.

On balance, our experience in Germany was a powerful and eye-opening time for us. The German Adventists were gracious, helpful, and incredibly generous. And we came to the place that we could discuss, even with much merriment, the differences between the friendly American, polite British, and thorough German approaches to life. Those are horrendous oversimplifications, but still remarkably accurate as generalizations.

In terms of my own experience, if Scotland introduced me to cultural diversity, Germany forced me to come to grips with differences in temperament. And as I have become more familiar with Ellen White's mature writings, I have discovered why she would celebrate such diversity as an asset, not a liability, especially if we seek to be the kind of worldwide body of Christ that our Lord has called us to be.

The Impact of Publishing and Signing Your Name (Church)

My first serious effort at publishing material about the growth and development of Ellen White came in the aftermath of Desmond Ford's famous challenge to the Adventist sanctuary doctrine. On October 27, 1979, before some one thousand people at an Adventist Forum meeting at Pacific Union College, Ford declared that it was "impossible" to prove the investigative judgment from the Bible.

When he delivered his fateful address, we were in Germany and thus missed out on the initial shock waves. While I had experienced my own struggles with the doctrine, I had worked the issues through to the point that it had become an important part of my theology. In brief, I no longer saw myself as standing in judgment as the accused, but as a witness to the goodness of God. The personal significance of that discovery, alluded to briefly in chapter 3, was so important to me, that I was not at all pleased by Ford's position.

But my curiosity was aroused. So I decided to find out how Ellen White supported the doctrine from Scripture. To my amazement, I discovered that *my* understanding of the investigative judgment simply wasn't there in her early publications, but was based on her later writings. I found significant differences between the two.

I ended up carefully comparing the first four chapters of *Patriarchs and Prophets* (1890) with the parallels in the two earlier sets, *Spiritual Gifts* (1858) and *Spirit of Prophecy* (1870). For me, the differences are striking, startling, and exciting. The published result was the five-part "Sinai to Golgotha" series, published in the *Adventist Review* in December of 1981, plus an additional piece on the investigative judgment, published in *Westwind,* the Walla Walla College alumni journal. The series presented both the biblical and Ellen White material in support of my fear-to-joy growth model. In short, I argued that Ellen White grew dramatically in her understanding of God and how He deals with human beings.

The response was so vigorous that the *Adventist Review* dedicated a whole issue to the discussion six months after the original series.[3] As events unfolded, I not only understood more about change and diversity in Ellen White's experience, but in the church as well.

In 1982, I proposed a book on the topic of "inspiration" to the Review and Herald. But Richard Coffen, then Book Editor at the Review, indicated that a book on the topic was already in process and had the support of the General Conference president. He gently suggested that I turn my energies elsewhere.

Then, in 1984, a proposed book review of George Rice's *Luke, A Plagiarist?* (1983)[4] turned into another series in the *Adventist Review,* this one a four-part series on inspiration, appearing in September 1985.[5]

That series, in turn, triggered an "official" invitation from the Review and Herald Publishing Association to write a book on inspiration. The other manuscript apparently had failed to materialize. I accepted. The Review published *Inspiration: Hard Questions, Honest Answers* in 1991.[6] It has now been translated by official church bodies into both German and Dutch.[7] The response to the book has been intense, both gratifying and troubling. But the discussion has been helpful for the church, I believe. The issues are now out on the table where they can be discussed and evaluated.[8]

Authority: Teacher and Academic Dean (College)

As a result of a remarkable series of events, I served as academic dean for four years at my home campus, Walla Walla College. Quite aside from my own contributions, it was a challenging time for the college. I jumped into the fray, eager to use my energies to fix everything that was wrong. Surprise! My high-energy approach succeeded in frightening many of my faculty colleagues. To make a long story short, I learned that I needed to be more patient, that I needed to be a better listener.

I also learned a great deal about how people relate to authority. Looking at myself in the mirror, I concluded that I have a great deal of respect for authority, but almost no fear of authority. Curiously, I had thought other people would relate to authority in the same way I did. Wrong. Having always been an outspoken faculty member, I assumed that I could continue in that style when I was dean. Wrong again. When I spoke as dean, people thought my word was law. I was almost as startled by their reaction as they were troubled by my outspokenness.

How does that apply to Ellen White and the Bible? I concluded that I am much more willing to "challenge" the traditional understanding of sacred texts than are most people. The questions I raise are all in a day's work for me; my confidence in God, in Scripture, and in Ellen White are actually enhanced by the freedom I feel to ask my questions. But I began to realize that my freedom may put other people's faith at risk. I think Brother Paul said something about that in 1 Corinthians 8 and 10. In any event, that was a very helpful thing to learn, almost making the "pain" of being dean worthwhile.

Personal: Discovering Strength in Weakness (Home)

If our stay in Germany forced me to recognize differences in temperament, two serious illnesses forced me to learn how to live with them, and that's because they didn't strike me, but my wife, Wanda. I will be brief but pointed here, since Wanda is a very private person. Her preference would be to say nothing at all. But if she thinks the story can possibly help others, she reluctantly grants permission for it to be told.

In 1979, toward the end of a very productive sabbatical in Scotland, Wanda came down with what was probably a form of viral encephalitis, at least that is what informed medical opinion now tells us. The remaining weeks of our stay there were difficult; her condition was probably more dangerous than we realized at the time. The lasting result has been dramatically reduced energy levels.

But there was more to come. The next summer (1980) when we were in Germany for the long-awaited teacher exchange, Wanda noticed what looked like an insect bite on her thigh. A German physician prescribed some ointment. In time, the rash disappeared, and life returned to normal. Normal for us, of course, meant grappling with her very limited energies. It wasn't until seven years later, however, that we discovered the "insect bite" was from a tick that had given her the gift of Lyme disease. The original diagnosis had been quite innocent since the medical community did not clearly link Lyme disease with its cause until 1984.

In 1987 Wanda began experiencing significant pain and swelling in her joints. She was on crutches for several months. Yet none of the standard medical tests revealed what was wrong. Finally, we went to a rheumatology specialist and long-time friend, Dr. Jerry Schoepflin. He had never seen a Lyme patient before; but he was well-read. In September of 1987 he suggested the possibility of Lyme disease and ordered a special blood test. The scale for that particular test was three for "weak positive" and seven for "strong positive." Wanda's reading came in at sixty-five!

The treatment was no fun, but we are grateful that the Lyme threat seems to have passed, even though the residual effect is very limited energy levels.

And what have we gained from it all? Three remarkable benefits, all illustrating the powerful truth that God is at work in all things to "bring about what is good."[9] (1) *Understanding illness.* Both of us learned a great deal about the long-term effects of serious illness. I have even begun to apply this knowledge to understanding my students. (2) *Discovering art.* Early in the diagnostic and treatment process, a doctor suggested to Wanda that she should explore low-energy options for finding fulfillment. Art? Good idea! Though Wanda had always loved art, Adventists, like conservative Christians in general, have tended to discourage in-depth interest in art because it is not "practical" enough. So she had never pursued it seriously. She had earned a B.S. in nursing, but felt that nursing wasn't for her. But now, on doctor's orders, so to speak, she set her sights on an art degree. One class a quarter over a six-year period brought her just that. In 1993 Walla Walla College granted her a B.A. in fine arts. For her, now, art not only brings her fulfillment on earth, but is probably her best window on God in heaven, too. (3) *Enriching marriage.* The combination of my high energy levels and her low ones have forced us to get to know each other a whole lot better than ever before. That's been good. Very good.

And where does Ellen White fit into all of this? I began hearing Ellen White's diversity statements like I had never heard them before. For example, "The trials of one are not the trials of another. The burdens that one finds light are to another most difficult and perplexing."[10]

Growth, Diversity and Change: Urgent Questions

Conservative believers typically find it very difficult to make peace with "diversity" and "change." Fears of "relativism" and "pluralism" loom large on the horizon. But our Adventist heritage offers us a marvelous opportunity, I believe, to encompass diversity and change in ways that can strengthen our most important convictions about God and His plans for us.

In my view, the root difficulty in two of the three questions noted below, the ones dealing with biblical interpretation and doctrinal stability, has to do with the misleading desire to find, both in Scripture and in the writings of Ellen White, divinely guaranteed *information* rather than divinely inspired means of *motivation.* Or, to put it another way, the desire for true facts and pure doctrine, rather than for right attitudes that will result in helpful service. In short, I have become convinced that the *truth of Scripture is rooted in its ethical and the moral aspects, not in the correctness of its raw facts and information.* The stability of the law pyramid is the great strength of the biblical (and Adventist) position. And because Adventists are committed to all of the Ten Commandments, including the Sabbath command, we have a consistent anchor that simply does not move: The one great principle of love, the two great commands, and the Ten Commandments are as enduring as the earth itself and are themselves rooted in eternal principles. That enables both simple and sophisticated people to worship and work together. We no longer have to quarrel over the differences between concrete and abstract perspectives on facts and information, because it is God's love, love for Him and for each other, that bonds us together. And that helps us focus directly on the third question below, the one dealing with the need for simplicity.

Here, then, are the three questions. In each case, a significant part of the response comes from the words of Ellen White, for that is how the very conservative author of this book was able to recognize and admit the truth that I thought I was beginning to see in Scripture and in her writings. I have asked these same questions, even with some urgency, and have found resolution. The challenge now is how to make them believable and acceptable to the larger church and world.

Question #1: **How can there be unity in the church if we allow for different interpretations and applications of the same passage of Scripture?**

If our first goal in studying Scripture is to find practical *applications* of the two great commands—love to God and love to one another—and effective *motivation* to help us realize the goals of these commands in our lives and in our world, then diverse interpretations and applications are not our enemies, but our friends. As documented in chapter 10, a fearful and melancholy young Ellen White in 1858 saw John the Baptist's austere life as being "without pleasure"; a self-confident and buoyant mature Ellen White in 1897 could look at the same simplicity and say that John "enjoyed" it. Our task is to find the right *use and application* of the story, not just to determine the right facts. On all counts, John lived a simple life. The intriguing question is whether or not he enjoyed it. When seen to be motivated by fear, it was no fun at all; but when seen to be motivated by gratitude and joy, the same simplicity became a delight.

It is helpful, but sobering, to note that in Adventism, the insistence on having one correct interpretation of Scripture has a troubling, but tenacious, history. In the turmoil over righteousness by faith that came to a crisis at the 1888 General Conference, President G. I. Butler was ready to set Adventist thinking in concrete, declaring in a circular letter to Adventist ministers that Adventists had "never taken a stand upon Bible exegesis which they have been compelled to surrender."[11]

In the same stormy setting of 1888, Uriah Smith took issue with A. T. Jones for suggesting that Adventists should change their interpretation of the tenth kingdom of Daniel 2 and 7 from the Huns to the Alemanni. Here is Smith's pointed comment to Jones:

> If the Huns are not to be reckoned as one of the ten, I think we are yet ten percent short on the fulfillment of Dan. 2 & 7. You can readily imagine what the effect would be, if our preachers, after presenting the ten kingdoms as they have for the past forty years, should now change upon a point which has been considered so well established, that it has never excited a dissenting voice, nor called forth a challenge from anyone. Thousands would instantly notice the change, and say: "Oh! now you find that you are mistaken on what you have considered one of your clearest points; and so if we give you time enough, you will probably come to acknowledge finally, that you are mistaken on everything." Thus the tendency would be to unsettle minds upon all points, a[nd] create confusion.[12]

When the same all-or-nothing view cropped up in connection with the 1888 General Conference session itself, Ellen White had blunt words to speak to those who held such a position:

> The remark was made, "If our views of Galatians are not correct, then we have not the third angel's message and our position goes by the board; there is nothing to our faith." I said, "Brethren, here is the very thing I have been telling you. This statement is not true. It is an extravagant, exaggerated statement. If it is made in the discussion of this question I shall feel it my duty to set this

6—E.F.T.F.

matter before all that are assembled, and whether they hear or forbear, tell them the statement is incorrect. The question at issue is not a vital question and should not be treated as such. The wonderful importance and magnitude of this subject has been exaggerated. For this reason—through misconception and perverted ideas—we see the spirit that prevails at this meeting, which is unchristlike, and which we should never see exhibited among brethren. There has been a spirit of Pharisaism coming in among us which I shall lift my voice against wherever it may be revealed. . . ." *And for the first time I began to think it might be we did not hold the correct views after all upon the law in Galatians, for the truth required no such spirit to sustain it.*

I returned to my room questioning what was the best course for me to pursue. Many hours that night were spent in prayer in regard to the law in Galatians. This was a mere mote. *Whichever way was in accordance with a "Thus saith the Lord," my soul would say, Amen, and Amen. But the spirit that was controlling our brethren was so unlike the spirit of Jesus, so contrary to the spirit that should be exercised toward each other, it filled my soul with anguish.*[13]

If we ask how Ellen White herself could take such a "loose" attitude toward the interpretation of Scripture, the answer can be found in the way she *shifts the focus from correct information to correct application, application of Jesus' two great commands.* Here is the significant quotation in which she makes that point with unmistakable clarity:

Christ prayed that His disciples might be one even as He and His Father are one. In what does this unity consist? This oneness does not exist because everyone has the same disposition, the same temperament, and thinks in the very same channel. All do not possess the same degree of intelligence. All have not the same experience. In a church there are different gifts and varied experiences. In temporal matters there are a great variety of ways of management, and yet these variations in manner of labor, in the exercise of gifts, do not create dissension, discord, and disunion.

One man may be conversant with the Scriptures, and some particular portion of the Scripture may be especially appreciated by him; another sees another portion as very important, and thus one may present one point, and another, another point, and both may be of highest value. This is all in the order of God. *But if a man makes a mistake in his interpretation of some portion of the Scripture, shall this cause diversity and disunion? God forbid. We cannot then take a position that the unity of the church consists in viewing every text of Scripture in the very same light. The church may pass resolution upon resolution to put down all disagreement of opinions, but we cannot force the mind and will, and thus root out disagreement. These resolutions may conceal the discord, but they cannot quench it and establish perfect agreement. Nothing can perfect unity in the church but the spirit of Christlike forbearance.* Satan can sow discord; Christ alone can harmonize the disagreeing elements. Then let every soul sit down in Christ's school and learn of Christ, who declares Himself to be meek and lowly of heart. Christ says that if we learn of Him, worries will cease and we shall find rest to our souls.

The great truths of the Word of God are so clearly stated that none need make a mistake in understanding them. When as individual members of the church, you love God supremely and your neighbor as yourself, there will be no need of labored efforts to be in unity, for there will be oneness in Christ as a natural result.[14]

Another 1888 manuscript allows us to be even more specific in illustrating her method, for in one instance she says outright that she does not consider some of E. J. Waggoner's interpretations of Scripture to be "correct"—yet goes right on to say that his message "harmonizes perfectly" with all that she has ever presented. How can she disagree and at the same time say that his message "harmonizes perfectly" with her view? By looking at focus and overall application, rather than on the detailed "factual" interpretation. Here are the significant paragraphs with the key lines highlighted:

Some interpretations of Scripture given by Dr. Waggoner I do not regard as correct. But I believe him to be perfectly honest in his views, and I would respect his feelings and treat him as a Christian gentle-man. I have no reason to think that he is not as much esteemed of God as are any of my brethren, and I shall regard him as a Christian brother, so long as there is no evidence that he is unworthy. The fact that he honestly holds some views of Scripture differing from yours or mine is no reason why we should treat him as an offender, or as a dangerous man, and make him the subject of unjust criticism. We should not raise a voice of censure against him or his teachings unless we can present weighty reasons for so doing and show him that he is in error. No one should feel at liberty to give loose rein to the combative spirit.

There are some who desire to have a decision made at once as to what is the correct view on the point under discussion. As this would please Elder B. [= G. I. Butler, General Conference president] it is advised that this question be settled at once. But are minds pre-pared for such a decision? I could not sanction this course, because our brethren are exercised by a spirit which moves their feelings, and stirs their impulses, so as to control their judgment. While un-der so much excitement as now exists, they are not prepared to make safe decisions.

I know it would be dangerous to denounce Dr. Waggoner's position as wholly erroneous. This would please the enemy. I see the beauty of truth in the presentation of the righteousness of Christ in relation to the law as the doctor has placed it before us. You say, many of you, it is light and truth. Yet you have not presented it in this light hereto-fore. Is it not possible that through earnest, prayerful searching of the Scriptures he has seen still greater light on some points? *That which has been presented harmonizes perfectly with the light which God has been pleased to give me during all the years of my experience.* If our ministering brethren would accept the doctrine which has been presented so clearly—the righteousness of Christ in connection with the law—and I know they need to accept this, their prejudices would not have a controlling power, and the people would be fed with their portion of meat in due season. Let us take our Bibles, and with humble prayer and a teachable spirit, come to the great Teacher of the world; let us pray as did David, "Open thou mine eyes, that I may behold wondrous things out of thy law" (Ps. 119:18).[15]

To sum up, the task of interpreting and applying Scripture must always be open to further guidance by the Spirit. God has given us a host of illustrations in Scripture for applying the one great principle of love, the two great commands, and the Ten Commandments. But all these illustrations and applications must "hang" on Jesus' two great commands (Matthew 22:40). All of us can strive for that goal, regardless of how simple or sophisticated, how bright or slow, we may be as individuals.

Question #2: If differences and changes in the interpretation of Scripture are allowed, won't that lead to changes in doctrine, something that would destroy the unity of the church?
The answer to the first part of the question is a clear "yes." Taking a fresh look at Scripture will affect how we understand doctrine, that is, the teachings of the church. But let us remember that the moral and ethical anchor never moves—the "One," the "Two," and the "Ten." Furthermore, the great events of biblical history never change—Creation, Fall, Flood, Exodus, monarchy, exile, restoration—all those are firmly in place in the Old Testament. Our interpretation of those events may change, but the events themselves are rooted in Scripture and history.

In the New Testament, the list is equally clear: Incarnation, Crucifixion, and Resurrection. And what stands at the end? What is the goal of it all? The hope of Jesus' return. But that is clearly a hope, not something we can "prove." Paul put it bluntly: "For in hope we were saved. Now hope that is seen is not hope. For who hopes for what is seen? But if we hope for what we do not see, we wait for it with patience."[16] In our modern scientific age, we are too often tempted to think that we need proof. Quite frankly, it's not there, and it won't work. The really essential elements in our Christian faith cannot be proven. The very attempt to prove them would destroy them. Faith, hope, and love, the big three from 1 Corinthians 13—how could you ever seek to "prove" any of these without destroying them? Faith, hope and love, are matters of trust, based on evidence, to be sure. But the evidence will always fall short of absolute proof.

If we are honest with all of Scripture, we will admit that the Old Testament's understanding of the end of time (eschatology) is not the same as that presented in the New Testament. Just compare Isaiah 65 and 66 and Zechariah 14 with Revelation 21 and 22. The point, the goal, is the same in both Testaments: God will come to restore His creation. But how He will do that and the understanding of the events that lead up to that restoration are seen quite differently.

The same could be said for the doctrine of God. The ideas of national deity and God's heavenly court that shape much of the Old Testament are several steps removed from the perspective of the New Testament. And our Trinitarian theology is much more sharply defined than anything we see in either Testament. Within Adventism, that is a point that is coming to light with greater clarity. Early Adventists did not accept the doctrine of the Trinity. Can James White and Uriah Smith still be part of God's kingdom? Of course. But they would not be comfortable with the full Trinitarian teaching modern Adventism now accepts.

But through all our differences, what holds us together is the advent hope—and the moral and ethical anchor of God's law. That's why I would be delighted if we could restore the early Adventist covenant to the head of our current statement of beliefs, the covenant used when Adventists first began organizing as a church:

> We, the undersigned, hereby associate ourselves together, as a church, taking the name, Seventh-day Adventists, covenanting to keep the commandments of God, and the faith of Jesus Christ [Rev. 14:12].[17]

The other aspect of the second question suggests that doctrinal diversity could fragment the church. It certainly has that potential. But it doesn't have to happen, not at all. Actually, it takes no talent at all to split the church. That's easy. Any difference of opinion can do the trick. The challenge is to keep the church together. In the words of Ellen White, quoted above: "Nothing can perfect unity in the church but the spirit of Christlike forbearance."[18] If we stay close to Christ, we will have lively debates about doctrine, but a tenacious unity as a result.

Question #3: How is it possible to maintain the simplicity of the faith with all the complexity introduced by growth, development, and change?

The end result of all this is actually amazingly simple. In their basic thrust, the "One," the "Two," and the "Ten" can be understood even by a small child. Even the fear-to-joy model is very simple. Paul put it this way to the Corinthians: "What would you prefer? Am I to come to you with a stick, or with love in a spirit of gentleness?"[19] But whether the means of motivation is tough or gentle, the ultimate goal is to do away with all external threats and bribes so that we may simply live in God's love. Could anything be more simple than that?

If we know that God loves us, the rest will fall into place. And He showed us His great love by taking on human flesh, living with us, dying, rising, and promising to come again. By grasping that great simplicity, Ellen White could exclaim with reference to John 3:16: "If one had no other text in the Bible, this alone would be a guide for the soul."[20]

Diversity: Bringing the Whole Church on Board[21]

The last step in this chapter and in this book is to take an honest look at the potential response of the church to the idea that Ellen White grew from fear to joy. In brief, the potential reactions are not all that different from the varied reactions to the tough stuff in the Old Testament as I noted in chapter 10: Some idolize the fearful parts, some idealize them, some avoid or ignore them, and some will be realistic, reading it all just as it is.

But for some, seeing the evidence for growth, change, and development in Ellen White's experience could put their faith at risk, even to the point that they will reject Ellen White, Adventism, Christianity, and God. Sadly, that has often happened in the last 150 years with reference to the Bible: For some, seeing what the Bible is *really* like when they expected something else, can lead to the loss of faith. I believe strong arguments can be marshaled to explain realistically how and why God has chosen to reveal Himself in Scripture—and in the writings of Ellen White. But it will take time for some to overcome their preconceived ideas of the way inspiration *should* function.

What follows, then, is a brief outline of the major potential responses, or at least *initial* responses to the idea that Ellen White grew from fear to joy in her experience and in her understanding of God. I have begun with atheism on the left (liberal) and moved step-by-step to Fundamentalism on the right (conservative). I see traces of all these positions, even the most radical ones, within the church. Based on my own experience, I am convinced that the fear-to-joy model can effectively bring us together as a church, a body of believers with a common faith and hope.

I should also explain my use of the words "liberal" and "conservative" in the descriptions that follow. In brief, within Adventism—and in the larger world as well—we use "liberal-conservative" as a matched pair in three basic ways: (1) The intellectual spectrum with the conservatives preferring clear-cut answers, and the liberals needing to ask their questions; (2) lifestyle spectrum with the conservatives seeking to resist the inroads of modern culture, and the liberals adapting to it; and (3) nearness-of-God spectrum with the conservatives sensing God's active presence in human life, and the liberals seeing God as more distant, impersonal, or detached. When taken to extremes, the conservative sense of God's personal presence can loom so large that it turns menacing; on the liberal side, the sense of a personal God can slip away completely, resulting in agnosticism and atheism.

In real life, the three ways of being liberal or conservative can be scrambled in a variety of ways. When all three line up on one side or the other, both the individual and the church could be at risk. In terms of generalizations, the forms of conservatism represented by the lifestyle and nearness-of-God perspectives are often found together.

For the record, I am an intellectual liberal because I must ask my questions. I am a lifestyle conservative because I believe Adventism's cautious approach to culture has brought many blessings my way and protected me from a host of dangers. Finally, on the nearness-to-God scale, I am solidly in the conservative camp, experiencing God's personal presence in a very real, albeit mysterious, way. And I am convinced that the "sense" of His presence has been a gift, not the result of anything I have done. In my earlier years it was a more threatening presence. But the story of Jesus has transformed the threat of His presence into a promise and reality of something that is encouraging, comforting, and hopeful. And for that I am grateful.

Here, then, is the list of potential responses to the idea that Ellen White "changed," growing from fear to joy in her understanding of God.

Attitudes Toward "Change" in EGW: From Atheism to Fundamentalism

1. Seeing the change, rejecting God and church (atheism). Those who abandon faith in God after seeing the differences in Ellen White's writings, do so because their idea of how God *should* inspire His messengers does not match what they actually see in her writings. Not all who adopt this position leave Adventism completely, though their residual ties would be largely cultural.

2. Seeing the change, but questioning if it comes from God (liberal, a more distant and impersonal God). A not-infrequent response from those of a lifestyle and intellectual liberal bent is that the really good things in Ellen White's later writings came from her secretaries, not from Ellen White herself. I have glimpsed this attitude from some who remain active in Adventism. But some who hold this perspective leave Adventism for more liberal churches on the left side of the religious spectrum.

3. Seeing the change as directed by God (moderate conservative). Those who see the change in Ellen White's experience and accept it as God's way of working are conservative in that they believe a personal God is directing her life; but, on the intellectual scale they are "liberal" by virtue of the fact that they have actually seen the differences at all.

4. Avoiding, ignoring, or idealizing the change (conservative, traditional mainstream). In general, official church publications have rarely distinguished between "early" and "late" in Ellen White's writings. At the level of the individual member, the general tendency has been to ignore, avoid, or idealize such changes. The reason for such reactions probably stems from the tendency of critics to present the evidence in a hostile and destructive way as a problem in itself, rather than as an exciting and practical way of "solving" the problem of the seemingly harsh and violent elements in Scripture and in the writings of Ellen White.

5. Seeing the change, but refusing to see it as coming from God; ignoring, avoiding, or idealizing the biblical parallels (conservative, leaving Adventism for other churches on the right side of the spectrum). Those who see the differences in the early and late Ellen White and leave Adventism for other churches typically are more conservative than the Adventist mainstream; often they refuse to use the same critical skills on the Bible that they willingly use to discredit Ellen White. Hence the response: "Don't you tear down my Bible to save Ellen White." My purpose in writing this book has been to show that the fear-to-joy model can be a great help in deepening our appreciation for both the Bible and the writings of Ellen White. For many reasons, I don't expect everyone in the church to be as excited as I am about the fear-to-joy model. But I do hope that it can be helpful to the church as a whole.

6. Seeing the change, but crediting the late material to the secretaries (conservative and Fundamentalist, sometimes leaving mainstream Adventism for independent Adventist organizations on the right). Those who prefer the hard-hitting early writings of Ellen White often view the more gentle later material as watered-down perversions by Ellen White's secretaries. These are the very devout and serious-minded believers who are most likely to identify with conservative independent Adventist groups who see the mainstream church as being in apostasy, or at least near apostasy.

Based on my own experience, I believe the fear-to-joy growth model does very well in meeting the needs of all these tendencies except the first one, the atheist. But even the atheist can see that we have been honest, and that may be a step in the right direction. Lifestyle and presence-of-God conservatives can conscientiously come on board because they can see God's hand at work. Intellectual and presence-of-God liberals can come on board too, but for a different reason. For them, simply being honest with all the evidence is what counts. The fear-to-joy model allows for a hierarchy of values; joy, the ultimate internal motivation, can clearly be seen as superior to the external motivation of fear. And that is crucial for the liberal.

Based on my own experience, I believe that seeing God's clear preference for positive motivation—joy instead of fear—makes it possible for us to be more buoyant, more energetic. At the risk of exaggerating, I'm tempted to say that I can do twice as much work and twice as effectively when I'm motivated by the positive side of God's love, instead of responding from fear. Maybe it's even as high as five times as much.

At the same time, however, I could regale you with stories of people who made their first step toward God only when a generous chunk of fear was in the mix. Not too long ago I was talking with an earnest young man whose life had been transformed in a charismatic service where the threat of an eternally burning hell was a key part of the story. He cleaned up his life and started keeping his promises. In other words, the fruits were positive. As he described the kind of preaching to which he and many others had responded, it was "Heaven sweet and hell hot!"

I don't believe Scripture teaches the doctrine of an eternal hell; still, there's plenty of fire in Scripture, even if it isn't eternal. Why? Some people need it in order to make the first step toward God. All that, of course, is one of the tragic results of sin. But God will reach people where they are, even scaring them into taking the first step toward Him.

Having said that, however, two points are important to note here. First, what I just described for you is indeed an intellectual "liberal" perspective—liberal on the intellectual scale, not on the presence-of-God scale. When it came to the willingness to ask hard questions, the mature Ellen White was an intellectual liberal, you see, and it is a message that could be preached only by a liberal. But God-fearing liberals who clearly sense God's presence—and thus are conservatives on the presence-of-God scale—are willing to live in both worlds, the joyful world of their own relationship with God, but also the fearful world of those who may need a touch of fear to turn them toward God. And maybe all of us need a touch of fear at least part of the time. That's why evangelism is so challenging—the human family is all over the place when it comes to motivation, a truth which the apostle Paul knew all about: "I have become all things to all people, that I might by all means save some."[22] My second point is a very practical one. Put simply, it is that we need both the early and the late Ellen White if we want to understand how God works, just as we need both Testaments in our Bible. That's true even if some things in the "early" or "old" scare us half to death! Somebody still needs that stuff.

In that connection, however, I do believe the church could pay more attention to dating Ellen White quotations. Recognizing the difference between "early" and "late" has been difficult for the church to admit, at least in print, even though there are subtle clues that even those who are not inclined to recognize the difference, still prefer her later writings. As I am writing this chapter, for example, it is with the awareness that the official White Estate Web site has made available online only a selection of her writings, all of them published after 1888. If you want to access *Testimonies for the Church,* you have to go to an "independent" site. *Testimonies for the Church* are still readily available at any Adventist Book Center and on disk. But they tend not to be high priority reading for "mainstream" Adventists. Perhaps that is the way it should be. But I would hope that we could at least be forthright in giving our reasons.

It is a major concern of mine in writing this book that we recognize the value of seeing the full Ellen White experience, both the early and the late, while clearly preferring the mature Ellen White's experience as being "better." In other words, if we have to choose, I would much prefer that the church Web site have the later writings rather than the earlier ones, though I do think it curious that one has to go to an independent site to access something as basic as *Testimonies for the Church.* Yet knowing something of what is in those volumes, especially the early ones, I can understand that too. For the most part, believers will select that which is helpful and simply leave to one side those things they do not understand or find less than helpful. After all, the Holy Spirit is still very alive and well, and knows how to work even where there are no books, no computers, no cell phones.

A Last Word on Diversity From Ellen White

In conclusion, I return to Ellen White's words on the importance of recognizing diversity. To Bible teachers she said:

> So today the Lord does not impress all minds in the same way. Often through unusual experiences, under special circumstances, He gives to some Bible students views of truth that others do not grasp. It is possible for the most learned teacher to fall far short of teaching all that should be taught.[23]

Too much diversity? She has a solution—come together in the presence of the Spirit:

> It would greatly benefit our schools if regular meetings were held frequently in which all the teachers could unite in the study of the word of God. They should search the Scriptures as did the noble Bereans. They should subordinate all preconceived opinions, and

taking the Bible as their lesson Book, comparing Scripture with Scripture, they should learn what to teach their students, and how to train them for acceptable service.[24]

And the last word? Once again, the opening lines in the chapter "In Contact With Others" from *The Ministry of Healing*:

> Every association of life calls for the exercise of self-control, forbearance, and sympathy. We differ so widely in disposition, habits, education, that our ways of looking at things vary. We judge differently. Our understanding of truth, our ideas in regard to the conduct of life, are not in all respects the same. There are no two whose experiences are[25] alike in every particular. The trials of one are not the trials of another. The duties that one finds light are to another most difficult and perplexing.
>
> So frail, so ignorant, so liable to misconception is human nature, that each of us should be careful in the estimate we place upon another.[26] We little know the bearing of our acts upon the experience of others. What we do or say may seem to us of little moment, when, could our eyes be opened, we should see that upon it depended the most important results for good or for evil.[27]

---

[1] The role of Ellen White has been at the eye of the storm in all the major "crises": Ron Numbers, author of *Prophetess of Health* (New York: Harper and Row, 1976; Knoxville: University of Tennessee Press, 1992), questioned Ellen White's inspiration because of her alleged dependence on nineteenth-century health reform sources. Numbers, a former Adventist and an academic, has moved away from faith on the left side of the spectrum.

Desmond Ford challenged the Adventist sanctuary doctrine, declaring that it is "impossible" to prove the investigative judgment from the Bible. The declaration was made at an Adventist Forum meeting on October 27, 1979, at Pacific Union College. In September 1980, the Australasian Division revoked Ford's ministerial credentials, but not his ordination. Ford has published his comprehensive presentation as *Daniel 8:14, The Day of Atonement, and the Investigative Judgment* (Casselberry, Fla.: Euangelion Press, 1980). For reports and comments on the proceedings that led to his loss of credentials, see *Spectrum* 11:2 (November 1980). Ford is still committed to Adventism and the Sabbath, but resigned his formal Seventh-day Adventist membership, held at the Pacific Union College Church, when he moved from the United States back to Australia in 2000.

Walter Rea, author of *The White Lie* (Turlock, Calif.: M & R Publications, 1982), formerly an Adventist pastor, challenged the Adventist understanding of inspiration in light of

Ellen White's use of undocumented sources in her published writings. Now retired and living in Patterson, California, Rea is still a committed Seventh-day Adventist; he simply believes the church has been wrong in its understanding of inspiration. Yet, in September 2004, he told me by phone: "If they put me behind the pulpit again, I would have no difficulty at all using Ellen White's devotional books, such as *The Desire of Ages, Christ's Object Lessons,* and *Steps to Christ.*"

Following Desmond Ford's lead in criticizing the investigative judgment, a number of (former) Adventists have moved further to the right on the religious spectrum, completely rejecting Adventism, the Sabbath, and Ellen White, but identifying with other Christian bodies, often in the reformed or charismatic tradition. In a rather flamboyant (and misleading) form, this position is represented in an anti-Adventist video, *Seventh-day Adventism: The Spirit Behind the Church.* Jeremiah Films, P.O. Box 1710, Hemet, CA 92546, 1998 [800-828-2290; <www.jeremiahfilms.com>]. The video features six former Adventist pastors: Mark Martin, Dale Ratzlaff, Sydney Cleveland, Wallace Slattery, Dave Snyder, and Dan Snyder.

An Adventist response is also available in video format: *Seventh-day Adventism: The Spirit Behind the Church: A Personal Response,* by Alden Thompson and Dave Thomas (March 2001), a one-hour video produced for and shown by Blue Mountain Television. Available for $17.00 from Blue Mountain TV, P.O. Box 205, College Place, WA 99324; 509-529-9149; email: manager@bluemttv.com.

One of the former Adventist pastors featured in the video, Dale Ratzlaff, has been particularly active in a ministry to former Adventists. Editor of *Proclamation,* a journal "For Former Adventists, Inquiring Adventists, Sabbatarians, Concerned Evangelicals," Ratzlaff has also published several books: *Sabbath in Crisis* (1989, 1995), reissued in 2003 as *Sabbath in Christ;* and *The Cultic Doctrine of Seventh-day Adventists* (1996). All Ratzlaff's titles are published by his Life Assurance Ministries, Glendale, Arizona: <www.ratzlaf.com>.

In addition to the Thomas-Thompson video response to the anti-Adventist video, other published responses (to Ratzlaff) include: Clifford Goldstein, *Graffiti in the Holy of Holies: An impassioned response to recent attacks on the sanctuary and Ellen White* (Nampa, Idaho: Pacific Press, 2003); Alden Thompson, "Conversations with the Other Side," *Spectrum* 31:4 (Fall 2003), pp. 54–59; and "Response to Dale Ratzlaff," *Ministry,* February 2004, pp. 30–32, 38. The Thompson pieces are also available on line at <www.aldenthompson.com>.

On the topic of diversity in Adventism, the following items are of interest, all available on the author's Web site: <www.aldenthompson.com>. "We Need Your Differences," *Adventist Review,* November 2, 1989, pp. 17–20; "Adventist Personality Types," *Insight,* August 10, 1985, pp. 6–11. Two unpublished pieces (similar in content) address diversity in the context of the post-Ford turmoil: "The Adventist Church at Corinth." Sabbath sermon, Walla Walla College Church, December 9, 1989. "The Adventists at Corinth and Their Favorite Preachers," chapter originally written for *Inspiration,* October 1991.

The author has also written several book review articles of books relevant to the discussion of inspiration, Ellen White, and doctrinal development, all of them published in *Spectrum,* all available on Thompson's Web site: <www.aldenthompson.com>.

Review of Walter Rea, *The White Lie* (Turlock, Calif.: M & R Publications, 1982): "The Imperfect Speech of Inspiration," *Spectrum* 12:4 (June 1982), pp. 48–55.

Review of George Rice, *Luke, A Plagiarist?* (Nampa, Idaho: Pacific Press, 1983): "Are Adventists Afraid of Bible Study?" *Spectrum* 16:1 (April 1985), pp. 56–60.

Review of Samuel Koranteng-Pipim, *Receiving the Word* (Berrien Springs, Mich.: Berean Books, 1996): "En Route to a 'Plain Reading' of Scripture," *Spectrum* 26:4 (January 1998), pp. 50–52.

Review of Herbert Douglass, *Messenger of the Lord: The Prophetic Ministry of Ellen G. White* (Nampa, Idaho: Pacific Press, 1998): "A Kinder, Gentler Ellen White," *Spectrum* 27:1 (Winter 1999), pp. 58–65.

Review of George Knight, *A Search for Identity: The Development of Seventh-day Adventist Beliefs* (Hagerstown, Md.: Review and Herald, 2000); Rolf Pöhler, *Continuity and Change in Christian Doctrine* (Frankfurt: Peter Lang, 1999); *Continuity and Change in Adventist Teaching* (Frankfurt: Peter Lang, 2000): " 'Gored by Every Sharp Tongue?' " *Spectrum* 29:3 (Summer 2001), pp. 68–71.

[2] For a more wide-ranging discussion, see Alden Thompson, *Inspiration: Hard Questions, Honest Answers* (Hagerstown: Review and Herald, 1991), chapter 7 ("God's Word: Casebook or Codebook?") and chapter 8 ("God's Law: The One, the Two, the Ten, the Many"), pp. 98–136. Also, Alden Thompson, *Who's Afraid of the Old Testament God?* (Gonzalez, Fla.: Pacesetters, 2003 [fourth ed.]), chapter 4, "Strange People Need Strange Laws," pp. 55–70.

[3] "From Sinai to Golgotha," five-part series in *Adventist Review,* December 3, 10, 17, 24, 31, 1981; additional article in *Westwind,* Walla Walla College alumni journal, "Even the Investigative Judgment Can Be Good News," *Westwind,* Winter, 1982, pp. 4–7, 11; follow-up issue of *Adventist Review,* July 1, 1982. See also "The Scary Lady of Adventism Learns to Have Fun," *Insight,* October 2, 1993, pp. 2–4; "From Burdensome Asceticism to Joyous Simplicity: The Interplay of Theology and Experience in the Life of Ellen White," paper presented for Pacific Northwest Region of AAR/SBL, Eugene, OR, May 5, 2002. All papers are available on the Web at <www.aldenthompson.com>.

[4] George Rice, *Luke, A Plagiarist?* (Nampa, Idaho: Pacific Press, 1983).

[5] September 5, 12, 19, 26, 1985, *Adventist Review*: "Adventists and Inspiration," September 5, 1985, pp. 5–7; "Improving the *Testimonies* through Revisions," September 12, 1985, pp. 13–15; "Questions and Perplexities without End," September 19, 1985, pp. 7–9; "Letting the Bible Speak for Itself," September 26, 1985, pp. 12–15. The *Adventist Review* articles are slightly shorter than the author's original versions which are available on his Web site: <www.aldenthompson.com>.

[6] The process by which the Review and Herald officially accepted *Inspiration* for publication was both thorough and wide-ranging. According to a telephone conversation with Richard Coffen (July 28, 1992), the Review and Herald typically invites six to ten people to review a manuscript. But for *Inspiration,* the Review invited fifty-seven people, fifty-one of them outside the Review and Herald itself. When the manuscript went to the book committee for a final vote, twenty-eight votes had been received, twenty-two in favor, six against. Though there were those who spoke against acceptance at the decisive committee meeting, when the final vote was taken, any who were still opposed apparently chose to abstain, for no negative votes were recorded. Coffen noted that the Review and Herald Book Committee at that time consisted of fifty-one members, twenty-six of whom were not employees of the Review.

[7] German edition: *Inspiration: Knifflige Fragen—Ehrliche Antworten.* Theologische Hochschule Friedensau, 1998. Dutch edition: *Inspiratie: Moeilijke vragen, eerlijke antwoorden.* Kerkgenootschap der Zevende-dags Adventisten, 2002.

[8] In 1992, the Adventist Theological Society published a collection of essays in response to *Inspiration*: Frank Holbrook and Leo Van Dolson, eds., *Issues in Revelation and Inspiration* (Berrien Springs, Mich.: Adventist Theological Society Publications, 1992). It consists of nine essays by eight Adventist scholars: Raoul Dederen, Samuel Koranteng-Pipim, Norman R. Gulley, Richard A. Davidson, Gerhard F. Hasel, Randall W. Younker, Frank Hasel, and Miroslav Kis. Free copies were sent to every Adventist church in North America. A German edition was published in 2000 under the title: *Offenbarung und Inspiration: Biblische Antworten auf knifflige Fragen.*

While the ATS volume focuses exclusively on *Inspiration,* Samuel Koranteng-Pipim's, *Receiving the Word* (Berrien Springs, Mich.: Berean Books, 1996) is more wide-ranging, challenging the positions adopted by *Inspiration* as well as those held by numerous other Adventist authors and church leaders. Pipim's book was privately published but later marketed by Review and Herald.

⁹ Romans 8:28, NIV, margin.

¹⁰ *The Ministry of Healing*, p. 483 (1905).

¹¹ "A Circular Letter to All State Conference Committees and Our Brethren in the Ministry" [January 1888], cited in George R. Knight, *Angry Saints* (Washington, D.C.: Review and Herald, 1989), p. 15.

¹² Uriah Smith to A. T. Jones, November 8, 1886, cited in George Knight, *Angry Saints* (Review and Herald, 1989), p. 20.

¹³ EGW Ms. 24, 1888 (EGW1888 1:220–223), emphasis supplied.

¹⁴ EGW Ms. 24, 1892 (EGW1888 3:1091–1093), emphasis supplied.

¹⁵ EGW Ms. 15, 1888 (EGW1888 1:164). Published in A. V. Olson, *Thirteen Crisis Years* [original title: *Through Crisis to Victory,* 1966] (Washington, D.C.: Review and Herald, 1981), p. 303.

¹⁶ Romans 8:24.

¹⁷ Adopted in 1861 at the organizing session of the first Seventh-day Adventist conference (Michigan), recommended for use in the organization of local churches; published in the *Review and Herald,* October 8, 1861. Cited from *The Seventh-day Adventist Encyclopedia* (1996), p. 416 ["Covenant, Church"].

¹⁸ EGW Ms. 24, 1892 (EGW1888 3:1092).

¹⁹ 1 Corinthians 4:21.

²⁰ *Testimonies to Ministers*, p. 370 (1896).

²¹ Though I have not developed the argument here, I am convinced that some of the modern forms of temperament analysis could significantly enhance our understanding of the diverse reactions in the church to ideas of "change" and "diversity." In particular, I am intrigued by the Myers-Briggs approach which is almost purely descriptive and non-judgmental. See, for example, David Keirsey, *Please Understand Me, II: Temperament, Character, Intelligence* (Del Mar, Calf.: Prometheus Nemesis Book Company, 1998).

²² 1 Corinthians 9:22.

²³ *Counsels to Parents and Teachers*, pp. 432, 433 (1913).

²⁴ *Ibid.*, p. 433 (1913).

²⁵ Original: "no two whose experience is alike."

²⁶ Original: "each should be careful in the estimate he places upon another."

²⁷ *The Ministry of Healing*, p. 483 (1905).

"Introduction" to *The Great Controversy* pp. v–xii

Before the entrance of sin, Adam enjoyed open communion with his Maker; but since man separated himself from God by transgression, the human race has been cut off from this high privilege. By the plan of redemption, however, a way has been opened whereby the inhabitants of the earth may still have connection with heaven. God has communicated with men by His Spirit, and divine light has been imparted to the world by revelations to His chosen servants. "Holy men of God spake as they were moved by the Holy Ghost." 2 Peter 1:21.

During the first twenty-five hundred years of human history, there was no written revelation. Those who had been taught of God, communicated their knowledge to others, and it was handed down from father to son, through successive generations. The preparation of the written word began in the time of Moses. Inspired revelations were then embodied in an inspired book. This work continued during the long period of sixteen hundred years—from Moses, the historian of creation and the law, to John, the recorder of the most sublime truths of the gospel.

The Bible points to God as its author; yet it was written by human hands; and in the varied style of its different books it presents the characteristics of the several writers. The truths revealed are all "given by inspiration of God" (2 Timothy 3:16); yet they are expressed in the words of men. The Infinite One by His Holy Spirit has shed light into the minds and hearts of His servants. He has given dreams and visions, symbols and figures; and those to whom the [v/vi] truth was thus revealed have themselves embodied the thought in human language.

The Ten Commandments were spoken by God Himself, and were written by His own hand. They are of divine and not of human composition. But the Bible, with its God-given truths expressed in the language of men, presents a union of the divine and the human. Such a union existed in the nature of Christ, who was the Son of God and the Son of man. Thus it is true of the Bible, as it was of Christ, that "the Word was made flesh, and dwelt among us." John 1:14.

Written in different ages, by men who differed widely in rank and occupation, and in mental and spiritual endowments, the books of the Bible present a wide contrast in style, as well as a diversity in the nature of the subjects unfolded. Different forms of expression are employed by different writers; often the same truth is more strikingly presented by one than by another. And as several writers present a subject under varied aspects and relations, there may appear, to the superficial, careless, or prejudiced reader, to be discrepancy or contradiction, where the thoughtful, reverent student, with clearer insight, discerns the underlying harmony.

As presented through different individuals, the truth is brought out in its varied aspects. One writer is more strongly impressed with one phase of the subject; he grasps those points that harmonize with his experience or with his power of perception and appreciation; another seizes upon a different phase; and each, under the guidance of the Holy Spirit, presents what is most forcibly impressed upon his own mind—a different aspect of the truth in each, but a perfect harmony through all. And the truths thus revealed unite to form a perfect whole, adapted to meet the wants of men in all the circumstances and experiences of life.

God has been pleased to communicate His truth to the world by human agencies, and He Himself, by His Holy Spirit, qualified men and enabled them to do this work. He guided the mind in the selection of what to speak and [vi/ vii] what to write. The treasure was entrusted to earthen vessels, yet it is, nonetheless, from Heaven. The testimony is conveyed through the imperfect expression of human language, yet it is the testimony of God; and the obedient, believing child of God beholds in it the glory of a divine power, full of grace and truth.

In His word, God has committed to men the knowledge necessary for salvation. The Holy Scriptures are to be accepted as an authoritative, infallible revelation of His will. They are the standard of character, the revealer of doctrines, and the test of experience. "Every scripture inspired of God is also profitable for teaching, for reproof, for correction, for instruction which is in righteousness; that the man of God may be complete, furnished completely unto every good work." 2 Timothy 3:16, 17, R.V.

Yet the fact that God has revealed His will to men through His word, has not rendered needless the continued presence and guiding of the Holy Spirit. On the contrary, the Spirit was promised by our Saviour, to open the word to His servants, to illuminate and apply its teachings. And since it was the Spirit of God that inspired the Bible, it is impossible that the teaching of the Spirit should ever be contrary to that of the word.

The Spirit was not given—nor can it ever be bestowed—to supersede the

Bible; for the Scriptures explicitly state that the word of God is the standard by which all teaching and experience must be tested. Says the apostle John, "Believe not every spirit, but try the spirits whether they are of God: because many false prophets are gone out into the world." 1 John 4:1. And Isaiah declares, "To the law and to the testimony: if they speak not according to this word, it is because there is no light in them." Isaiah 8:20.

Great reproach has been cast upon the work of the Holy Spirit by the errors of a class that, claiming its enlightenment, profess to have no further need of guidance from the word of God. They are governed by impressions which they regard as the voice of God in the soul. But the spirit [vii/viii] that controls them is not the Spirit of God. This following of impressions, to the neglect of the Scriptures, can lead only to confusion, to deception and ruin. It serves only to further the designs of the evil one. Since the ministry of the Holy Spirit is of vital importance to the church of Christ, it is one of the devices of Satan, through the errors of extremists and fanatics, to cast contempt upon the work of the Spirit and cause the people of God to neglect this source of strength which our Lord Himself has provided.

In harmony with the word of God, His Spirit was to continue its work throughout the period of the gospel dispensation. During the ages while the Scriptures of both the Old and the New Testament were being given, the Holy Spirit did not cease to communicate light to individual minds, apart from the revelations to be embodied in the Sacred Canon. The Bible itself relates how, through the Holy Spirit, men received warning, reproof, counsel, and instruction, in matters in no way relating to the giving of the Scriptures. And mention is made of prophets in different ages, of whose utterances nothing is recorded. In like manner, after the close of the canon of the Scripture, the Holy Spirit was still to continue its work, to enlighten, warn, and comfort the children of God.

Jesus promised His disciples, "The Comforter which is the Holy Ghost, whom the Father will send in My name, He shall teach you all things, and bring all things to your remembrance, whatsoever I have said unto you." "When He, the Spirit of truth, is come, He will guide you into all truth: . . . and He will show you things to come." John 14:26; 16:13. Scripture plainly teaches that these promises, so far from being limited to apostolic days, extend to the church of Christ in all ages. The Saviour assures His followers, "I am with you alway, even unto the end of the world." Matthew 28:20. And Paul declares that the gifts and manifestations of the Spirit were set in the church "for the perfecting of the saints, for the work of the ministry, for the edifying of the body of Christ: till we all come in the unity of the faith, and of the knowledge [viii/ix] of the Son of God, unto a

perfect man, unto the measure of the stature of the fullness of Christ."
Ephesians 4:12, 13.

For the believers at Ephesus the apostle prayed, "That the God of our Lord
Jesus Christ, the Father of glory, may give unto you the *Spirit of wisdom and
revelation* in the knowledge of Him: *the eyes of your understanding being enlight-
ened;* that ye may know what is the hope of His calling, and . . . what is the
exceeding greatness of His power to usward who believe." Ephesians 1:17-19.
The ministry of the divine Spirit in enlightening the understanding and opening to the mind the deep things of God's holy word, was the blessing which
Paul thus besought for the Ephesian church.

After the wonderful manifestation of the Holy Spirit on the Day of Pentecost, Peter exhorted the people to repentance and baptism in the name of
Christ, for the remission of their sins; and he said: "Ye shall receive the gift of
the Holy Ghost. For the promise is unto you, and to your children, and to all
that are afar off, even as many as the Lord our God shall call." Acts 2:38, 39.

In immediate connection with the scenes of the great day of God, the
Lord by the prophet Joel has promised a special manifestation of His Spirit.
Joel 2:28. This prophecy received a partial fulfillment in the outpouring of
the Spirit on the Day of Pentecost; but it will reach its full accomplishment
in the manifestation of divine grace which will attend the closing work of the
gospel.

The great controversy between good and evil will increase in intensity to
the very close of time. In all ages the wrath of Satan has been manifested against
the church of Christ; and God has bestowed His grace and Spirit upon His
people to strengthen them to stand against the power of the evil one. When
the apostles of Christ were to bear His gospel to the world and to record it for
all future ages, they were especially endowed with the enlightenment of the
Spirit. But as the church approaches her final deliverance, Satan is to work
with greater power. He comes down "having great wrath, because he knoweth
that he hath but a [ix/x] short time." Revelation 12:12. He will work "with all
power and signs and lying wonders." 2 Thessalonians 2:9. For six thousand
years that mastermind that once was highest among the angels of God has
been wholly bent to the work of deception and ruin. And all the depths of
satanic skill and subtlety acquired, all the cruelty developed, during these
struggles of the ages, will be brought to bear against God's people in the final
conflict. And in this time of peril the followers of Christ are to bear to the
world the warning of the Lord's second advent; and a people are to be prepared
to stand before Him at His coming, "without spot, and blameless." 2 Peter
3:14. At this time the special endowment of divine grace and power is not less
needful to the church than in apostolic days.

Through the illumination of the Holy Spirit, the scenes of the long-continued conflict between good and evil have been opened to the writer of these pages. From time to time I have been permitted to behold the working, in different ages, of the great controversy between Christ, the Prince of life, the Author of our salvation, and Satan, the prince of evil, the author of sin, the first transgressor of God's holy law. Satan's enmity against Christ has been manifested against His followers. The same hatred of the principles of God's law, the same policy of deception, by which error is made to appear as truth, by which human laws are substituted for the law of God, and men are led to worship the creature rather than the Creator, may be traced in all the history of the past. Satan's efforts to misrepresent the character of God, to cause men to cherish a false conception of the Creator, and thus to regard Him with fear and hate rather than with love; his endeavors to set aside the divine law, leading the people to think themselves free from its requirements; and his persecution of those who dare to resist his deceptions, have been steadfastly pursued in all ages. They may be traced in the history of patriarchs, prophets, and apostles, of martyrs and reformers. [x/xi]

In the great final conflict, Satan will employ the same policy, manifest the same spirit, and work for the same end as in all preceding ages. That which has been, will be, except that the coming struggle will be marked with a terrible intensity such as the world has never witnessed. Satan's deceptions will be more subtle, his assaults more determined. If it were possible, he would lead astray the elect. Mark 13:22, R.V.

As the Spirit of God has opened to my mind the great truths of His word, and the scenes of the past and the future, I have been bidden to make known to others that which has thus been revealed—to trace the history of the controversy in past ages, and especially so to present it as to shed a light on the fast-approaching struggle of the future. In pursuance of this purpose, I have endeavored to select and group together events in the history of the church in such a manner as to trace the unfolding of the great testing truths that at different periods have been given to the world, that have excited the wrath of Satan, and the enmity of a world-loving church, and that have been maintained by the witness of those who "loved not their lives unto the death."

In these records we may see a foreshadowing of the conflict before us. Regarding them in the light of God's word, and by the illumination of His Spirit, we may see unveiled the devices of the wicked one, and the dangers which they must shun who would be found "without fault" before the Lord at His coming.

The great events which have marked the progress of reform in past ages are matters of history, well known and universally acknowledged by the Protestant world; they are facts which none can gainsay. This history I have presented briefly, in accordance with the scope of the book, and the brevity which must necessarily be observed, the facts having been condensed into as little space as seemed consistent with a proper understanding of their application. In some cases where a historian has so grouped together [xi/xii] events as to afford, in brief, a comprehensive view of the subject, or has summarized details in a convenient manner, his words have been quoted; but in some instances no specific credit has been given, since the quotations are not given for the purpose of citing that writer as authority, but because his statement affords a ready and forcible presentation of the subject. In narrating the experience and views of those carrying forward the work of reform in our own time, similar use has been made of their published works.

It is not so much the object of this book to present new truths concerning the struggles of former times, as to bring out facts and principles which have a bearing on coming events. Yet viewed as a part of the controversy between the forces of light and darkness, all these records of the past are seen to have a new significance; and through them a light is cast upon the future, illumining the pathway of those who, like the reformers of past ages, will be called, even at the peril of all earthly good, to witness "for the word of God, and for the testimony of Jesus Christ."

To unfold the scenes of the great controversy between truth and error; to reveal the wiles of Satan, and the means by which he may be successfully resisted; to present a satisfactory solution of the great problem of evil, shedding such a light upon the origin and the final disposition of sin as to make fully manifest the justice and benevolence of God in all His dealings with His creatures; and to show the holy, unchanging nature of His law, is the object of this book. That through its influence souls may be delivered from the power of darkness, and become "partakers of the inheritance of the saints in light," to the praise of Him who loved us, and gave Himself for us, is the earnest prayer of the writer.

Selected Messages, Book 1, pp. 15–23
The Inspiration of the Prophetic Writers

The Inspiration of the Word of God

This is a time when the question with all propriety may be asked, "When the Son of man cometh, shall he find faith on the earth?" (Luke 18:8).

Spiritual darkness has covered the earth and gross darkness the people. There are in many churches skepticism and infidelity in the interpretation of the Scriptures. Many, very many, are questioning the verity and truth of the Scriptures. Human reasoning and the imaginings of the human heart are undermining the inspiration of the Word of God, and that which should be received as granted, is surrounded with a cloud of mysticism. Nothing stands out in clear and distinct lines, upon rock bottom. This is one of the marked signs of the last days.

This Holy Book has withstood the assaults of Satan, who has united with evil men to make everything of divine character shrouded in clouds and darkness. But the Lord has preserved this Holy Book by His own miraculous power in its present shape—a chart or guidebook to the human family to show them the way to heaven.

But the oracles of God have been so manifestly neglected that there are but few in our world, even of those [15/16] who profess to explain it to others, who have the divine knowledge of the Scriptures. There are learned men who have a college education, but these shepherds do not feed the flock of God. They do not consider that the excellencies of the Scriptures will be continually unfolding their hidden treasures as precious jewels are discovered by digging for them.

There are men who strive to be original, who are wise above what is written; therefore, their wisdom is foolishness. They discover wonderful things in advance, ideas which reveal that they are far behind in the comprehension of the divine will and purposes of God. In seeking to make plain or to unravel mysteries hid from ages from mortal man, they are like a man floundering about in the mud, unable to extricate himself and yet telling others how to get out of the muddy sea they themselves are in. This is a fit representation of the men who set themselves to correct the errors of the Bible. No man can improve the Bible by suggesting what the Lord meant to say or ought to have said.

Some look to us gravely and say, "Don't you think there might have been some mistake in the copyist or in the translators?" This is all probable, and the mind that is so narrow that it will hesitate and stumble over this possibility or probability would be just as ready to stumble over the mysteries of the Inspired Word, because their feeble minds cannot see through the purposes of God. Yes, they would just as easily stumble over plain facts that the common mind will accept, and discern the Divine, and to which God's utterance is plain and beautiful, full of marrow and fatness. All the mistakes will not cause trouble to one soul, or cause any feet to stumble, that would not manufacture difficulties from the plainest revealed truth.

God committed the preparation of His divinely inspired Word to finite man. This Word, arranged into books, the Old and New Testaments, is the guidebook to the inhabitants of a fallen world, bequeathed to them that, by studying and obeying the directions, not one soul would lose its way to heaven. [16/17]

Those who think to make the supposed difficulties of Scripture plain, in measuring by their finite rule that which is inspired and that which is not inspired, had better cover their faces, as Elijah when the still small voice spoke to him; for they are in the presence of God and holy angels, who for ages have communicated to men light and knowledge, telling them what to do and what not to do, unfolding before them scenes of thrilling interest, waymark by waymark in symbols and signs and illustrations.

And He [God] has not, while presenting the perils clustering about the last days, qualified any finite man to unravel hidden mysteries or inspired one man or any class of men to pronounce judgment as to that which is inspired or is not. When men, in their finite judgment, find it necessary to go into an examination of scriptures to define that which is inspired and that which is not, they have stepped before Jesus to show Him a better way than He has led us.

I take the Bible just as it is, as the Inspired Word. I believe its utterances in an entire Bible. Men arise who think they find something to criticize in God's Word. They lay it bare before others as evidence of superior wisdom. These men are, many of them, smart men, learned men, they have eloquence and talent, the whole lifework [of whom] is to unsettle minds in regard to the inspiration of the Scriptures. They influence many to see as they do. And the same work is passed on from one to another, just as Satan designed it should be, until we may see the full meaning of the words of Christ, "When the Son of man cometh, shall he find faith on the earth?" (Luke 18:8).

Brethren, let not a mind or hand be engaged in criticizing the Bible. It is a work that Satan delights to have any of you do, but it is not a work the Lord has pointed out for you to do.

Men should let God take care of His own Book, His living oracles, as He has done for ages. They begin to question some parts of revelation, and pick flaws in the apparent inconsistencies of this statement and that state- [17/18] ment. Beginning at Genesis, they give up that which they deem questionable, and their minds lead on, for Satan will lead to any length they may follow in their criticism, and they see something to doubt in the whole Scriptures. Their faculties of criticism become sharpened by exercise, and they can rest on nothing with a certainty. You try to reason with these men, but your time is lost. They will exercise their power of ridicule even upon the Bible. They even become mockers, and they would be astonished if you put it to them in that light.

Brethren, cling to your Bible, as it reads, and stop your criticisms in regard to its validity, and obey the Word, and not one of you will be lost. The ingenuity of men has been exercised for ages to measure the Word of God by their finite minds and limited comprehension. If the Lord, the Author of the living oracles, would throw back the curtain and reveal His wisdom and His glory before them, they would shrink into nothingness and exclaim as did Isaiah, "I am a man of unclean lips, and I dwell in the midst of people of unclean lips" (Isa. 6:5).

Simplicity and plain utterance are comprehended by the illiterate, by the peasant, and the child as well as by the full-grown man or the giant in intellect. If the individual is possessed of large talents of mental powers, he will find in the oracles of God treasures of truth, beautiful and valuable, which he can appropriate. He will also find difficulties, and secrets and wonders which will give him the highest satisfaction to study during a long lifetime, and yet there is an infinity beyond.

Men of humble acquirements, possessing but limited capabilities and opportunities to become conversant in the Scriptures, find in the living oracles comfort, guidance, counsel, and the plan of salvation as clear as a sunbeam. No one need be lost for want of knowledge, unless he is willfully blind.

We thank God that the Bible is prepared for the poor man as well as for the learned man. It is fitted for all ages and all classes.—Manuscript 16, 1888 (written at Minneapolis, Minn., in autumn of 1888). [18/19]

Objections to the Bible

Human minds vary. The minds of different education and thought receive different impressions of the same words, and it is difficult for one mind to give to one of a different temperament, education, and habits of thought by language exactly the same idea as that which is clear and distinct in his own mind. Yet to honest men, right-minded men, he can be so simple and plain as to convey his meaning for all practical purposes. If the man he communicates with is not honest and will not want to see and understand the truth, he will turn his words and language in everything to suit his own purposes. He will misconstrue his words, play upon his imagination, wrest them from their true meaning, and then entrench himself in unbelief, claiming that the sentiments are all wrong.

This is the way my writings are treated by those who wish to misunderstand and pervert them. They turn the truth of God into a lie. In the very same way that they treat the writings in my published articles and in my books, so do skeptics and infidels treat the Bible. They read it according to their desire to pervert, to misapply, to willfully wrest the utterances from their true meaning. They declare that the Bible can prove anything and everything, that every sect proves their doctrines right, and that the most diverse doctrines are proved from the Bible.

The writers of the Bible had to express their ideas in human language. It was written by human men. These men were inspired of the Holy Spirit. Because of the imperfections of human understanding of language, or the perversity of the human mind, ingenious in evading truth, many read and understand the Bible to please themselves. It is not that the difficulty is in the Bible. Opposing politicians argue points of law in the statute book, and take opposite views in their application and in these laws.

The Scriptures were given to men, not in a continuous chain of unbroken utterances, but piece by piece through successive generations, as God in His providence saw a fitting opportunity to impress man at sundry times and [19/20] divers places. Men wrote as they were moved upon by the Holy Ghost. There is "first the bud, then the blossom, and next the fruit," "first the blade, then the ear, after that the full corn in the ear." This is exactly what the Bible utterances are to us.

There is not always perfect order or apparent unity in the Scriptures. The miracles of Christ are not given in exact order, but are given just as the circumstances occurred, which called for this divine revealing of the power of Christ. The truths of the Bible are as pearls hidden. They must be searched, dug out by painstaking effort. Those who take only a surface view of the Scriptures will, with their superficial knowledge, which they think is very deep, talk of the contradictions of the Bible, and question the authority of the Scriptures. But those whose hearts are in harmony with truth and duty will search the Scriptures with a heart prepared to receive divine impressions. The illuminated soul sees a spiritual unity, one grand golden thread running through the whole, but it requires patience, thought, and prayer to trace out the precious golden thread. Sharp contentions over the Bible have led to investigation and revealed the precious jewels of truth. Many tears have been shed, many prayers offered, that the Lord would open the understanding to His Word.

The Bible is not given to us in grand superhuman language. Jesus, in order to reach man where he is, took humanity. The Bible must be given in the language of men. Everything that is human is imperfect. Different meanings are expressed by the same word; there is not one word for each distinct idea. The Bible was given for practical purposes.

The stamps of minds are different. All do not understand expressions and statements alike. Some understand the statements of the Scriptures to suit their own particular minds and cases. Prepossessions, prejudices, and passions have a strong influence to darken the understanding and confuse the mind even in reading the words of Holy Writ.

The disciples traveling to Emmaus needed to be disentangled in their interpretation of the Scriptures. Jesus [20/21] walked with them disguised, and as a man He talked with them. Beginning at Moses and the prophets He taught them in all things concerning Himself, that His life, His mission, His sufferings, His death were just as the Word of God had foretold. He opened their understanding that they might understand the Scriptures. How quickly He straightened out the tangled ends and showed the unity and divine verity of the Scriptures. How much men in these times need their understanding opened.

The Bible is written by inspired men, but it is not God's mode of thought and expression. It is that of humanity. God, as a writer, is not represented. Men will often say such an expression is not like God. But God has not put Himself in words, in logic, in rhetoric, on trial in the Bible. The writers of the Bible were God's penmen, not His pen. Look at the different writers.

It is not the words of the Bible that are inspired, but the men that were inspired. Inspiration acts not on the man's words or his expressions but on the man himself, who, under the influence of the Holy Ghost, is imbued with thoughts. But the words receive the impress of the individual mind. The divine mind is diffused. The divine mind and will is combined with the human mind and will; thus the utterances of the man are the word of God.—Manuscript 24, 1886 (written in Europe in 1886).

Unity in Diversity

There is variety in a tree, there are scarcely two leaves just alike. Yet this variety adds to the perfection of the tree as a whole.

In our Bible, we might ask, Why need Matthew, Mark, Luke, and John in the Gospels, why need the Acts of the Apostles, and the variety of writers in the Epistles, go over the same thing?

The Lord gave His word in just the way He wanted it to come. He gave it through different writers, each having his own individuality, though going over the same history. Their testimonies are brought together in one Book, and [21/22] are like the testimonies in a social meeting. They do not represent things in just the same style. Each has an experience of his own, and this diversity broadens and deepens the knowledge that is brought out to meet the necessities of varied minds. The thoughts expressed have not a set uniformity, as if cast in an iron mold, making the very hearing monotonous. In such uniformity there would be a loss of grace and distinctive beauty. . . .

The Creator of all ideas may impress different minds with the same thought, but each may express it in a different way, yet without contradiction. The fact that this difference exists should not perplex or confuse us. It is seldom that two persons will view and express truth in the very same way. Each dwells on particular points which his constitution and education have fitted him to appreciate. The sunlight falling upon the different objects gives those objects a different hue.

Through the inspiration of His Spirit the Lord gave His apostles truth, to be expressed according to the development of their minds by the Holy Spirit. But the mind is not cramped, as if forced into a certain mold.—Letter 53, 1900.

The Lord Speaks in Imperfect Speech

The Lord speaks to human beings in imperfect speech, in order that the degenerate senses, the dull, earthly perception, of earthly beings may comprehend His words. Thus is shown God's condescension. He meets fallen human beings where they are. The Bible, perfect as it is in its simplicity, does not answer to the great ideas of God; for infinite ideas cannot be perfectly embodied in finite vehicles of thought. Instead of the expressions of the Bible being exaggerated, as many people suppose, the strong expressions break down before the magnificence of the thought, though the penman selected the most expressive language through which to convey the truths of higher education. Sinful beings can only bear to look upon a shadow of the brightness of heaven's glory.—Letter 121, 1901. [22/23]

No Man to Pronounce Judgment on God's Word

Both in the [Battle Creek] Tabernacle and in the college the subject of inspiration has been taught, and finite men have taken it upon themselves to say that some things in the Scriptures were inspired and some were not. I was shown that the Lord did not inspire the articles on inspiration published in the Review,* neither did He approve their endorsement before our youth in the college. When men venture to criticize the Word of God, they venture on sacred, holy ground, and had better fear and tremble and hide their wisdom as foolishness. God sets no man to pronounce judgment on His Word, selecting some things as inspired and discrediting others as uninspired. The testimonies have been treated in the same way; but God is not in this.—Letter 22, 1889.

---

* Reference here is to a series of articles the writer of which advocated that there were "differences in degrees" of inspiration. See *The Review and Herald*, Jan. 15, 1884.—Compilers

Index of Bible Passages Cited

Index of Ellen White References Cited

If you enjoyed this book, you'll enjoy these as well:

The Prophet and Her Critics
Leonard Brand and Don McMahon examine the accusations of Ellen White's most vocal critics who say she borrowed the health message. Other questions about inspiration, 19th-century health reforms, and more are also addressed in this important new book.
0-8163-2057-8. Paperback.
US$11.99, Can$17.99.

Messenger of the Lord
Herbert Douglass. A comprehensive look at the gift of prophecy as manifested in the life and work of Ellen White. This book deals candidly with the issues raised in recent years and sets forth abundant reasons for affirming her claim to be God's messenger.
0-8163-1622-8. Hardcover. US$24.99, Can$37.49.

Graffiti in the Holy of Holies
Clifford Goldstein. This book dissects the arguments being leveled at the investigative judgment and the Spirit of Prophecy revealing solid ground for our faith in both. This may be Goldstein's most important book in a decade. A must-read for every Adventist.
0-8163-2007-1. Paperback.
US$12.99, Can$19.49.

Order from your ABC by calling **1-800-765-6955**, or get online and shop our virtual store at **www.AdventistBookCenter.com**.
- Read a chapter from your favorite book
- Order online
- Sign up for email notices on new products